Stephen Pollan's

FOOLPROOF GUIDE

to Selling Your Home

STEPHEN M. POLLAN
& MARK LEVINE

ILLUSTRATIONS BY BETSY BAYTOS

A FIRESIDE BOOK
PUBLISHED BY SIMON & SCHUSTER
NEW YORK LONDON TORONTO
SYDNEY TOKYO SINGAPORE

FIRESIDE
Rockefeller Center
1230 Avenue of the Americas
New York, NY 10020

FIRESIDE and colophon are registered trademarks
of Simon & Schuster, Inc.

DESIGNED BY BARBARA M. MARKS

Manufactured in the United States of America

2 4 6 8 10 9 7 5 3 1

Library of Congress Cataloging-in-Publication Data
Pollan, Stephen M.
Stephen Pollan's foolproof guide to selling your home /
Stephen M. Pollan & Mark Levine.
p. cm.
"A Fireside book."
Includes index.
1. House selling—United States.   I. Levine, Mark, 1958–
II. Title.
HD259.P65   1996
333.33'83—dc20   95-36642
                                                            CIP

ISBN: 0-684-80229-5

CONTENTS

BECOME A SERIOUS SELLER

Ten years ago you didn't need a book to help you sell your home. That was because the process was almost automatic. Sellers listed their home with a broker, started getting offers right away, shook hands on a deal within a month, paid off their mortgage, and pocketed the profits . . . which were often substantial. Certainly, no one ever lost money when they sold their home. My, how times have changed!

Today the sale of a home is a major pro-

duction. In fact, by the end of the process you'll feel like Cecil B. DeMille must have after he finished shooting *The Ten Commandments*. The residential real estate market has gone through a revolution in the past decade. Now, homes don't automatically increase in value—in fact, they may not even retain their value. Rather than being besieged by hordes of eager buyers, today's home seller can often count the number of potential buyers on the fingers of one hand. And those select few are all very picky shoppers. Homes are now on the market for a minimum of three months; some, unfortunately, are on the market for as long as three years. Rather than pocketing handsome profits, today's home seller considers himself lucky if he gets back what was paid for the home.

I'm probably not telling you anything you don't already know. After all, you've picked up this book for a reason. But here's something you may not have focused on yet: this is not a temporary change in fortune, a momentary shift to a buyer's market that you can wait out. Selling a home will remain problematic for the foreseeable future. That's because of America's demographics.

Real estate prices rose dramatically during the 1970s and 1980s because baby boomers were looking for homes. The 76 million individuals who make up the largest generation in American history drove up the prices of property. Simply put, there were more willing buyers than there were homes available. The fundamental laws of supply and demand took over and drove prices up. Boomers, who generally grew up in homes their parents owned, saw real estate ownership as one of the foundations for their financial lives. They were doing well financially, since the economy was booming. They were ready, willing, and able to pay a premium to replicate the lives their parents had led.

Now, by and large, baby boomers are no longer shopping for homes. In fact, the older members of the generation, who are now reaching middle age, are beginning to think about selling. They're finding the market dynamics have changed. The new generation of buyers is very small. The economy may be doing well right now, but the recession of the late 1980s and early 1990s shattered illusions that it would always grow. Widespread corporate layoffs have cast a shadow over plans for the future. Today, there are far fewer buyers than there are homes for sale, and those buyers are reluctant to spend too much. The result? Homes are selling at a discount rather than a premium price.

Clearly, there's nothing you can do about these facts. Sure, it's a bad break for you; a really bad break if you bought when the market was high. But cursing fate won't change things. Actually, it will just make things worse because you'll be wasting time. The answer is to take charge of the situation. You can sell your home. Let me repeat that: YOU CAN SELL YOUR HOME! I know because I sell homes all the time.

Actually, I help my clients sell homes. I'm an attorney and financial adviser whose practice has involved the buying and selling of real estate for more than three decades. I've helped clients sell everything from multimillion-dollar estates to two-bedroom cottages. It's not a boast to say that after more than thirty years in this business I've seen it all. And if there's one fundamental thing I've learned about selling real estate it's that there's no such thing as a problem property—there are only problem sellers.

I'll be offering literally hundreds of tips and warnings in this book—some that apply to those selling single-family homes, others that apply to those selling apartments, and most that apply to all home sellers—but the single most important piece of advice I can offer you is this: You must have a seller's attitude.

Far too many people say they're ready to sell when they're not. They say they want to sell their home . . . for the right price. Of course, that price offers them a substantial profit, substantial enough to either buy another home or to support them in retirement. A serious seller wants to sell his or her home . . . period. He or she accepts that the price obtained for the home is primarily contingent on the real estate market in general, and only partly determined by the specific characteristics of his or her house. Sure, there are lots of things a seller can do to *maximize* how much he or she gets for the home—and I'll be going over all of them in this book. But there's nothing an individual seller can do to change the real estate market. If you want to sell your home you must accept that there are certain things *beyond* your power. The most obvious of these is its general value range.

That having been said, a serious seller also resolves to do everything that is *within* his or her power to get top dollar for the home. He or she doesn't let personal taste or emotion stand in the way of the sale. From the day he or she decides to sell, all the emotions wrapped up in the home are set aside and it becomes a commodity. Rather than trying to sell his or her tastes, the seller resolves to turn the home into a mirror that will reflect the taste of whoever is looking at it. And just as important, the serious seller realizes that time is money.

Once you decide to sell your home, every day it isn't sold is another day's interest you've lost. Serious sellers do everything they can to sell quickly in order to get those dollars in their bank earning interest. That means they're ready to make a deal with the first person who makes an offer.

Finally, serious sellers understand that they can't sell their homes alone. Like it or not, a serious seller hires a real estate broker and experienced attorney and accepts that their commission and fees are just two more costs of selling for top dollar, quickly.

By following the step-by-step process outlined in the following pages, by using the tips offered, and by heeding the warnings issued, you *will* be able to sell your home for the most money possible, as quickly as possible. And that, after all, is the true goal of any serious seller. It's not going to be easy and it won't happen overnight. But take it from me, if you follow this program, it will happen.

—*Stephen M. Pollan*

How to Use This Book

This book is designed to be used, not just read. The project of selling your home, and it *is* a project with a beginning, middle, and end, has been broken down into a series of eight stages. Each of these stages has then been broken down into an easy-to-follow series of steps. Tips and warnings about each step are also provided. Before acting on any individual step, read through the book, including all the tips and warnings, once. Then, go back to the beginning and proceed through the process, using the book as a guide. When you complete a step, check the box labeled "done," and move on to the next step. Avoid the temptation to jump ahead or to do things out of order. The stages and steps have been designed to build on one another and have been written based on more than thirty years' experience of going through this exact process. —*Stephen M. Pollan*

GET YOUR TIMING DOWN

The most overlooked part of the entire home-selling process is working out the timing of the whole transaction. While most people know that late spring and early summer are the best times to sell, few bother to get the ball rolling early enough so both they and their house are truly ready by prime time. The goal of this initial stage is to help you create a customized time line designed to insure you'll be fresh on the market when buyers are the hungriest.

1 Circle April on your calendar. The prime time for selling homes is the spring. That's because it's the only time of year when there's pressure on buyers. Anyone with kids wants to have them settled in time for the first day of school in September. That means they start looking in April and continue through the spring and early summer. An added bonus is that most homes look best this time of year when the sun is shining and plants are in bloom. Your goal then is to have your house ready to be listed on April 1.

☐ **Done**

2 Begin calculating how long it will take you to get your house ready.

In order to insure you get top dollar and sell quickly, you need both a fully prepared home and an April 1 debut. Therefore, you need to figure out if the former will allow the latter.

☐ **Done**

3 Do your own buyer's inspection.

To sell your home quickly, you need to insure that it is as unobjectionable as possible. To do that, inspect your home—inside and outside—with a critic's eye . . . just as a potential buyer will. Look for any aesthetic or minor mechanical problems. Is there a crack on the wall? Is the carpet frayed? Is the wallpaper peeling? Are there stains from old leaks? Does a door stick? Is there a broken window? Are any surfaces or fixtures cracked or chipped? Do all cabinets, doors, and drawers have working knobs and handles? Do all the lights work? Make a checklist of everything that needs repair.

☐ **Done**

TIP 3.1: Sometimes after living in a home for a while you can become oblivious to its problems. Ask a friend to help you conduct an inspection of your house. Just make sure you tell them it's vital they be as blunt as possible. If you have a pal who's particularly picky, use him: now is the time when his fastidiousness can pay off for you.

TIP 3.2: Make sure to check places not in the line of sight. Just because a defect is hidden, that doesn't mean it won't be spotted. Assume the buyers (or their inspector) will have the detective skills of Sherlock Holmes. For instance, look up. Are there cracks in the ceiling paint, or stains from a leak upstairs? Don't forget to move furniture and look under it. Is the couch covering carpet stains or hiding damaged baseboard moldings?

TIP 3.3: Similarly, check rooms you rarely use. Is the basement, attic, or crawl space a burial ground for broken toys? Do out-of-the-way areas smell musty or moldy?

WARNING 3.4: While you're conducting your own inspection, start compiling a little history of your home. Savvy home shoppers will be asking your broker for lots of information. You must be able to provide the broker good answers to all their questions. Here are some typical questions you can expect your broker will have to field:
• Has the basement leaked within the past three years? If so, were repairs made?
• What type of roof does the house have? How old is it? Has it leaked within the past three years? If so, were repairs made?
• Has the plumbing

system backed up within the past three years? If so, were repairs made?

• What type of heating/cooling system does the house have? How old is it? Are all rooms serviced by it? How many zones are there? When was it last repaired or serviced?

• What are the average monthly bills for electricity, gas, fuel/oil, and water?

• Does the fireplace work? When was it last repaired or serviced?

• Are there storms and screens for every window and door?

• What type of flooring is under the areas covered by carpeting?

• Are the gutters and downspouts in need of repair? When were they last cleaned?

• What is the capacity of the hot-water heater? How old is it? When was it last serviced or repaired?

• What type of electrical service does the home have? Do fuses blow or circuit breakers trip when more than one appliance is in use?

• Are the exterior walls and attic and basement ceilings insulated?

• Do all the door locks work and will keys be provided for each?

• Has there ever been a termite problem? How was the problem treated and are there ongoing inspections?

4 Hire an inspector and have a formal inspection done.

Most buyers have a home inspected prior to closing the deal. Problems uncovered then become part of the negotiation. Either the selling price is reduced by the cost of the repair, or the seller is asked to make the repair prior to closing. Since you'll be going through this process anyway, it makes sense to do it prior to putting the home on the market. That way you can either take action now to clear up potential trouble, or set an accurate price that reflects existing problems.

☐ **Done**

TIP 4.1: Make sure the inspector you hire is a licensed engineer or home inspector, and is certified to spot insect infestation. Assume that an inspection by a professional will cost you from $100 to $300 depending on the size of your home.

TIP 4.2: Your attorney can recommend a certified home inspector. Or, call the American Society of Home Inspectors at (708) 290-1919 and ask for a list of members in your area. Members of this association must meet stringent training criteria and live up to a strict code of ethics and conduct.

WARNING 4.3: Your home engineer/inspector can also test for a variety of environmental problems, but these tests carry further charges. A radon-gas test usually costs $100 to $125. Testing household water for lead or bacteria can run between $75 and $125. Inspecting well water for hardness, magnesium, copper, and bacteria will cost about an additional $150.

WARNING 4.4: Some environmental hazard tests—such as looking for lead content in paint, determining whether in-ground fuel tanks are leaking, or checking for electromagnetic fields from high-tension wires—must be done by specialists. Your home engineer will be able to offer recommendations.

WARNING 4.5: While your home engineer will be able to point out materials that appear to contain asbestos, he or she will not be able to make a definitive judgment. You can, however, ask him or her to recommend a specialist to examine and test the material.

5

Decide if your house will need any substantial outside renovation or repair work. If your preinspection shows that substantial outside work—such as roof patching, landscaping, or outside painting—needs to be done, you may have two problems. First, any substantial work requires a certain amount of time, time that you may not have if you want to be ready for April. Second, outside work needs to be done in the early spring, at the latest. So if you need to have the house painted for the market in April, and it's already January, you've got an automatic problem, regardless of how long the work will take.

☐ **Done**

Decide if your house will need any substantial inside renovation or repair work. If your preinspection shows that substantial inside work—such as painting or floor sanding—needs to be done, your only problem is whether or not there's sufficient time to have it done prior to April.

☐ **Done**

TIP 6.1: Substantial in both these cases refers to work that you can't do yourself part-time, work that should be done by a professional. For instance, you may be able to repair the wallpaper in a single room or touch up the railing by your front steps effectively, but you probably won't have time to paint the walls and ceilings in three rooms and still get everything else accomplished. Likewise, only a professional has the ability to sand and seal the wood floors in the living room and dining room and have it look top-notch.

7 Speak with contractors and find out how long the necessary work will take.

Ask friends and neighbors to recommend three contractors for each job. Check their references and past work, and then solicit bids, stressing that time is of the essence. From the estimates you're given, calculate whether you can have the work done by April.

☐ **Done**

TIP 7.1: Be willing to pay a little more for work that will be done promptly. Remember that the additional cost of having the house ready for April may well be outweighed by the interest you could earn on the proceeds from the prompt sale of your home for top dollar. Pay the additional amount on timely completion.

8 **Decide if you need substantial cosmetic work done on the interior or exterior.** If you need substantial cosmetic changes, such as adding light fixtures, window treatments, cleaning carpets, refinishing fixtures, or having an industrial cleaning job done, figure that you'll need another thirty to sixty days to get ready.

☐ **Done**

TIP 8.1: Substantial cosmetic work refers to projects that, while not time-consuming, will require hiring a professional and/or selecting and buying fixtures.

9 **Decide how much minor cosmetic work you need done.** Doing things like sanitizing the house, thinning out furniture and the contents of closets, upgrading and replacing lightbulbs, and silencing door squeaks will take anywhere from one week to two weeks, depending on how much work needs to be done and how willing you are to devote all your free time to the task.

☐ **Done**

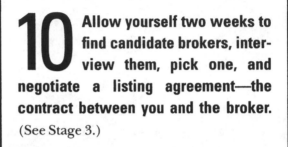

10

Allow yourself two weeks to find candidate brokers, interview them, pick one, and negotiate a listing agreement—the contract between you and the broker.
(See Stage 3.)

☐ **Done**

11 Allow yourself one week to study comparables (a record of recent sales in your area for homes substantially similar to yours), look at other homes on the market, and set a price range. (See Stage 5.)

☐ **Done**

12 Allow yourself two weeks for developing your marketing plan and putting it in place. (See Stage 5.)

☐ **Done**

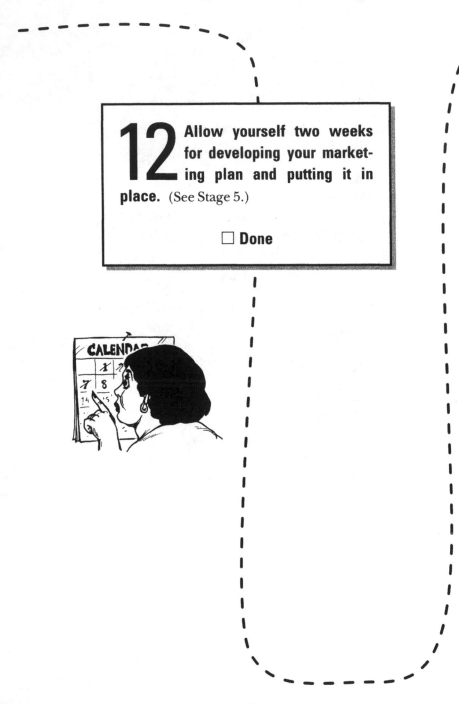

13 Allow yourself two weeks to find candidate attorneys, select one, and prepare him or her for rapid action. (See Stage 3.)

☐ **Done**

14

Search your soul and measure your motivation. If you're not willing to focus all your spare time—that means every evening after work and most of the day on weekends—to the task of getting your house ready for prime selling season, add another two weeks to your time line.

☐ **Done**

15

Begin thinking about where you will be moving to—if you haven't already. You don't need to decide where you'll be moving to if you don't already know. And you certainly don't need to start looking for a new home yet. (It's always better to sell first, and then buy, since you eliminate being under any time pressure.) However, now is the time to start thinking about it . . . in what little spare time you have.

☐ **Done**

16 Figure out your starting date.

Take out your calendar. Using that circled April 1 as your goal, work backward, adding weeks for all the work and tasks you've determined you need to do in order to get your house ready for market. If you aren't behind schedule already, that's great. Get started tomorrow and you'll be able to take a couple of evenings off.

☐ **Done**

TIP 16.1: If you're a month or less behind schedule, that's not a big deal. If you work extra hard you can still probably get your home on the market before the end of April. You may miss some early-bird shoppers, but you'll be fine.

17

If you won't be able to have your house ready, you'll need to pick the lesser of three evils. Your choices are to schedule the work, but accept that you'll get less for your home since it won't be on the market during the prime selling season; not have the work done, but accept that you'll get less for your home since it won't be in prime condition; or delay the sale for a year in the hope that an improved market and condition will compensate for the lost interest resulting from the delay.

☐ **Done**

TIP 17.1: Be aware that good marketing can somewhat make up for bad timing. If you choose to put the house on the market during the off-season, you'll simply need to intensify marketing efforts. (See Stage 5.)

PREPARE THE
HOUSE FOR LISTING

Now that you've got your timing
down, the next stage in the home-
selling process is to make your home
as unobjectionable as possible to potential buyers, and therefore, as attractive as
possible for brokers. You'll add the special
touches that will make it stand out from
the crowd later. For now, your goal is to
insure there's nothing wrong with your
home.

18

Sanitize your house. Before you show your home to anyone, even a broker, it must be given a spring cleaning to end all spring cleanings. A clean home, regardless of any other trait, will get compliments from buyers. They'll believe—rightly or wrongly—that a clean home means a well-maintained home, and will feel more comfortable about moving in. Pay particular attention to walls, windows, rugs, and carpets.

☐ **Done**

TIP 18.1: If you're going to do the cleaning yourself here are some things to remember. Of course, start with the basics: vacuum, wash and/or polish floors, dust, and wash windows. Pay special attention to the bathrooms and kitchen. Clean fixtures inside and out, using vinegar, diluted bleach, or baking soda to remove any mildew. Finally, make sure to go the extra mile. Dust pictures hanging on the walls. Take books and other items on display off shelves and dust them, as well as the shelf. Dust or vacuum blinds. Wash curtains or drapes. Clean radiators and the floor behind them.

TIP 18.2: If you've neither the time nor the muscles to do a thorough cleaning job, hire a service to do the job for you. Every dollar you spend having the home cleaned will be repaid with two dollars added to your bottom line. Top-notch residential cleaning services usually charge $10 to $12 per hour, with a minimum of three to four hours. If you need what's called "heavy cleaning," the fee rises to between $15 and $18 per hour. Supplies are often extra.

TIP 18.3: If parts of the house need the attention of cleanup specialists—perhaps there has been a flood in the basement or carpeting and upholstery are terribly stained—contact your insurance agent and ask for the name of a local service that cleans up after fires and floods. These restoration services charge by the square foot, and have various prices for carpeting, walls, and furniture.

19 Toss out all unwanted items.

Most of us are pack rats. We tend to accumulate more than we need and fill up whatever storage areas are available. While that sometimes makes a home feel warmer, it also makes rooms, closets, and cabinets seem smaller. Go through all your furnishings, accessories, clothes, and housewares with an eye toward eliminating anything you can to make the house seem larger. Your goal is to make your home look like a suite in a fine hotel.

☐ **Done**

TIP 19.1: If you can't bear to sell unnecessary furniture, create the illusion of spaciousness by putting it in storage until your home is sold.

TIP 19.2: If your floors are in good shape, consider removing rugs and carpeting. Sweeping vistas of wood, vinyl, or tile flooring, uninterrupted by rugs or carpets, make rooms look twice as large.

TIP 19.3: Rearrange furniture to improve traffic flow through your home. The last thing you want is for buyers to think your house is small and cramped. Push furniture as far back toward the walls as you can without making it look obvious. Just make sure doors are able to open fully.

WARNING 19.4: Overcrowded walls can make a room appear much smaller than it really is.

TIP 19.5: Conquer your closets by thinning them out. Go through your clothes, getting rid of any you've outgrown or that are no longer in style. Store off-season clothing in the basement or attic. Hang a shoe rack on the back of the closet door to free up space on the floor, and make sure shelves are well organized and neat. Every closet should feature its own light—if yours don't have them already, closet lights can be purchased at the hardware store. Finally, invest in a sachet or potpourri for each closet in your home.

TIP 19.6: Never underestimate the use of underbed storage boxes. Not only can they help you keep closets clutter free, but they're also convenient for when brokers want to bring buyers over on short notice and you need to tidy up pronto.

TIP 19.7: Get the most out of your garage by cleaning it up! Maximize space by hanging things like bicycles, gardening tools, snow shovels, and toboggans from the walls or ceiling. Remove any debris and wash any auto drippings off the floor. A single coat of deck paint on the floor will make the space seem larger and cleaner. If you hold your household trash in the garage while waiting for it to be picked up, make sure the odors are well contained.

TIP 19.8: Hold a yard sale before selling your home, not after. Getting rid of useless clutter will make storage spaces appear larger and give your home a neater appearance.

WARNING 19.9: If you have second thoughts about going through this thinning-out process, either for reasons of senti-ment or time, look at it this way: You're going to have to do it before you pack up to move anyway. If you do it now you'll also make some money on the deal.

20

Clean and repair your floors. Make sure carpets are clean and free of stains, and vinyl, wooden, and tile floors are polished. If there are any easily fixed cracks or gaping seams, fix them. If they can't be fixed, consider adding area or throw rugs, as long as they don't look out of place.

☐ **Done**

TIP 20.1: You can revive the color of a rug by vacuuming it and then applying a solution of one part white vinegar and three parts boiling water. Dampen just the nap of the rug, not the backing. When it's dry, rub it with dry bread crumbs and vacuum once again.

TIP 20.2: Scratches in vinyl flooring can often be erased by rubbing them with a soft cloth moistened with paste floor wax. If that doesn't work, try rubbing the scratch with the edge of a coin. If even that doesn't work, put two layers of aluminum foil over the scratch and press it with a hot iron.

WARNING 20.3: Never wash wooden floors with water. They can warp or rot. Instead, use a special wood cleaner or polish.

TIP 20.4: Repair squeaky floors. You might find the squeaks charming, especially if your home is older, but buyers aren't likely to agree. If your floors "speak," pull loose floorboards tight with screws inserted below. If you don't have access to floors from below, ring-shanked nails driven in from above will do the trick. Wooden floors are notoriously creaky. If yours are problematic, drill some tiny pilot holes to prevent the wood from splitting, then hammer in some finish nails at a forty-five-degree angle to grab the subfloor.

Alternating the direction of the nails will give you the best grip. If the cause of the squeak is a warped or bowed floor joist, look for movement between the joists and bridging when weight is placed upon it, then fill those spaces with wood shims.

TIP 20.5: Repair squeaky stairs. Try screwing down the tread or putting in wedges from below. Simply gluing a squeaky tread sometimes works.

WARNING 20.6: Shabby stair treads can hurt the appearance of your home. If you haven't done so already, clean the carpeting on your stairs. If it's beyond hope, consider tearing it up to see what the bare steps beneath have to offer. Wooden steps that are in good shape might only require a light waxing. Those in older homes are most likely painted, in which case you need only add another coat of paint.

21 Repaint walls and repair wallpaper.

Don't think you'll be able to get away with touching up damaged areas. That will just signal to buyers that there's a problem underneath. Instead, have a good, one-coat paint job done with heavy-duty, semigloss, off-white. This will show the best and offend no one. Repaint scuffed stair treads and risers, too. It's not worth hanging new wallpaper, however. Instead, patch any loose seams and do the best you (or a professional paperhanger) can to make it look presentable.

☐ **Done**

TIP 21.1: To make a long, dark hall appear brighter, consider wallpapering with a vertical-striped pastel pattern. Or at least think about hanging a few pictures: they will catch shoppers' eyes and minimize the tunnel effect. If nothing else, consider hanging a large, well-placed mirror to create the illusion of more space.

WARNING 21.2: Make sure rooms that are sun hungry are not painted a dark color. If they are, repaint walls white, increase the wattage of your lightbulbs, and hang sheer curtains.

TIP 21.3: You can make a small kitchen appear larger by painting the walls, ceiling, and cabinets white. The uniformity of color will give the walls and ceiling the appearance of receding, which opens up the space to the eye. Consider removing curtains completely, as well.

22

Check all your kitchen appliances. Make sure your kitchen appliances are spotless inside and out and are in working order. It's not worth replacing any, but it is worth repairing them, or replacing worn-out parts.

☐ **Done**

TIP 22.1: If you want to get a nice shine on your appliances, try rubbing them with a piece of wax paper.

TIP 22.2: If the finish of your appliances is chipped, look for matching porcelain paint. If you can't find it, look for matching touch-up paint at either an auto parts store or a hobby shop. Typewriter correction fluid often works well, too.

TIP 22.3: The least expensive and quickest way to fix large chips and cracks in appliance exteriors is with an epoxy resin. Check with your local hardware store for recommendations and instructions.

TIP 22.4: If the racks in your oven, or the broiler tray, are soiled beyond even the most intensive scouring, consider replacing them with new ones. The same goes for the spill pans for your stove's burners, any soiled racks in your dishwasher, and broken bins in your refrigerator.

TIP 22.5: A very inexpensive way to dress up an otherwise average appliance is to replace the exterior hardware. Knobs, handles, and even faceplates can be purchased at a good appliance repair store.

TIP 22.6: While you're busy cleaning your refrigerator inside and out, get rid of as much of the food inside it as you can. Just as thinning out closets makes them look bigger, so will tossing out that five-year-old, half-empty jar of marmalade, and other unnecessary items. By the way, the emptier your refrigerator and freezer are, the easier it will be for the buyer to see how clean—and valuable—the appliance is.

WARNING 22.7: Small appliances can crowd kitchen counters, giving the impression of inadequate space. To avoid this, store them out of sight when your home is being shown, including your drying rack and any bottles of dishwashing liquid that may clutter the sink area.

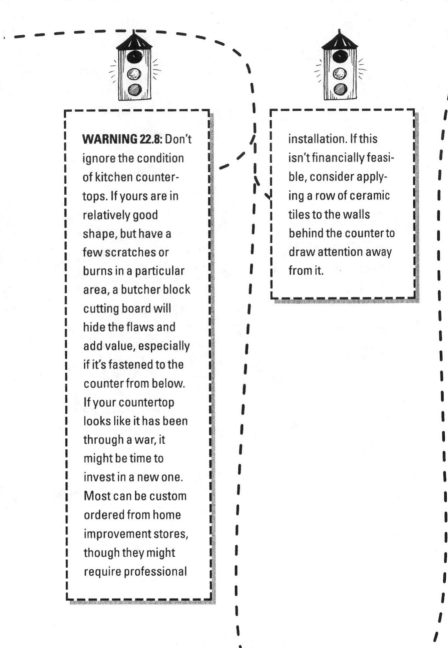

WARNING 22.8: Don't ignore the condition of kitchen countertops. If yours are in relatively good shape, but have a few scratches or burns in a particular area, a butcher block cutting board will hide the flaws and add value, especially if it's fastened to the counter from below. If your countertop looks like it has been through a war, it might be time to invest in a new one. Most can be custom ordered from home improvement stores, though they might require professional installation. If this isn't financially feasible, consider applying a row of ceramic tiles to the walls behind the counter to draw attention away from it.

23

Restore your bathroom to tip-top shape. It's probably too expensive to have a professional repair your porcelain fixtures. It's certainly too expensive to replace them. Instead, check the warehouse-style, home do-it-yourself stores for repair kits. Make sure you get rid of rust stains. Soaking the area with white vinegar works well. Similarly, don't bother regrouting tiles, just get rid of any mildew with vinegar, diluted bleach, or baking soda.

☐ **Done**

TIP 23.1: One of the simplest and cheapest ways to dress up a bathroom is simply to buy a new white shower curtain and hooks, and a new, white wooden toilet seat.

TIP 23.2: Rubbing alcohol will clean the vinyl caulking around bathtubs and sinks. It also does a good job on chrome and glass.

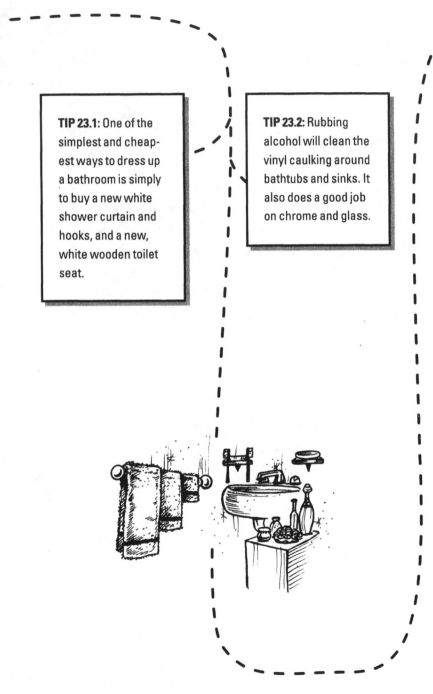

24

Don't neglect your basement. You could have the most beautiful home in the world, but if your basement is dank and musty-smelling, chances are buyers are going to turn tail. Start by cleaning and organizing yours. If you have basement windows, wash them. Erase all signs of dampness by getting rid of mildew stains as well as any old furniture that might be maintaining that musty odor. If there has ever been a flood in your basement—as evidenced by high water marks on the walls—repaint the walls. Make sure the entire area is well lit, and remember to wipe down your water heater and furnace. It'll help them look newer.

☐ **Done**

TIP 24.1: Almost every basement has a damp smell, even if there's no actual water problem. Consider picking up a dehumidifier and keeping it on before and during the time your home is on the market. If you're asked about it, you can explain its presence by saying you hang your laundry up in the basement. If you have a clothes rack nearby it will help.

TIP 24.2: Many home maintenance catalogs sell room deodorizers consisting of small mesh pouches containing volcanic ash. Hiding them in the corners of the basement will eliminate odors without adding telltale signs of your efforts.

TIP 24.3: The basement (like the garage) often becomes the graveyard for broken or outgrown toys and games. Get rid of as many as you can. Those with sentimental value should be stored in a toy chest.

25

Don't neglect your attic. Dark, dingy attics can detract from a house's charm. Whether yours is huge or barely a crawl space, make sure it's clean and cobweb free. Most important of all, make sure it's well lit. Replace existing bulbs with new ones of a higher wattage. If the attic isn't wired for electricity, have the work done. And, just as you've done in the rest of the house, get rid of any materials you don't plan on taking with you. Rearrange those that remain in as neat and unobtrusive a manner as possible.

☐ **Done**

TIP 25.1: If your attic is big enough to use as an extra room, convey this to buyers through the creative use of props: a well-placed train set might help them to envision a playroom, for example. Use what you've got.

TIP 25.2: Another way to demonstrate the utilitarian potential of attic space is to install rods between ceiling beams for hanging out-of-season garments.

26

Trim and clean your landscaping. Remember you're not just selling your home—you're also selling the property that goes with it. You won't recoup the cost of relandscaping, but cleaning and tidying up will pay off in a higher price, quicker—especially if you'll be selling in prime time, when flowers are in bloom. Make sure your lawn is mowed regularly and neatly edged where grass meets the sidewalk or driveway. Seed any bare spots. Trim bushes back into discernible shapes. Remove overhanging tree branches.

☐ **Done**

TIP 26.1: The best attitude to take toward yard preparations is to act as if you were going to be holding a garden party in your yard . . . and inviting your boss.

WARNING 26.2: Pot-holed, weed-filled driveways spell neglect. Make sure your driveway is beyond reproach. While you need not resurface the whole driveway, at least repair cracks, fill in potholes if possible, pull up weeds, and make sure all toys are out of sight. If you're showing your home in the winter, make sure the drive is shoveled, with plenty of sand or rock salt down so that no one slips.

WARNING 26.3: If you've let your dog do its business in your yard, clean it up and stop! If a buyer soils his or her shoe walking around the yard, your home won't be remembered kindly.

TIP 26.4: Just as it's worth hiring someone to clean your home if you're not up to the task, it's also worth hiring someone to spruce up your yard. Have trees and bushes pruned. Flower boxes and beds should be planted with hearty annuals like marigolds or impatiens. During winter months, beds should be covered—pine boughs are much more appealing than hay—if only to give the impression that a beautiful garden lies below, waiting to bloom come spring. If nothing else, consider hiring a professional gardener to do the initial work, and let your local teenage neighbor do the maintenance for as long as your home is on the market.

TIP 26.5: Upgrade your fence. If it's an old chain-link fence that has started to rust, remove the rust with a wire brush and then paint the fence dark green. If you have a stockade fence, or if your chain-link is in relatively good shape, add some colorful plants to draw attention from the fence itself. Also keep in mind that buyers look to a fence to provide privacy. If your chain-link fence doesn't fit the bill, look into attaching a canvas cloth to it. Canvas generally runs about $1.50 per square foot and comes in a variety of colors. Just make sure you order it with grommets so you can tie it to the fence easily.

TIP 26.6: Know your property's boundaries. Yards that are clearly delineated by a hedge or fence present no problem. But if your boundary markings are obscure, get yourself some wooden stakes, paint them a bright color, and sink them into the ground at the corners of your property.

27 Make sure your home has curb appeal.

First impressions do count. Make sure the walk leading to your front door is safe, clean, well lit, and manicured. The numbers on your home should be visible from the street. Your mailbox should be cosmetic as well as functional. And your doorbell must work, too.

☐ **Done**

WARNING 27.1: Don't forget about the roof and gutters. Loose shingles and leaky downspouts convey neglect. Make sure your gutters are cleaned of debris and leaks are patched. Replace damaged, loose, or blistered shingles.

WARNING 27.2: If your house has peeling paint or if it is a color you love, but that doesn't fit the environment (pink and turquoise, while perfect for Florida or southern California, look out of place in New England), a paint job is in order. There's no need to get fancy—just go for a basic white, off-white, or gray color. Fix broken shutters and replace any missing. Opt for a simple complimentary color, like black. Loose siding should be nailed into place. Rotten wood clapboards should be replaced. Mildewed metal or vinyl siding should be cleaned.

TIP 27.3: If your home has a front porch, put out a couple of pieces of furniture to create a homey feeling. Just make sure they are in good condition. Remove clutter, such as toys and gardening tools. Put the flags away— they're just as likely to annoy as they are to attract.

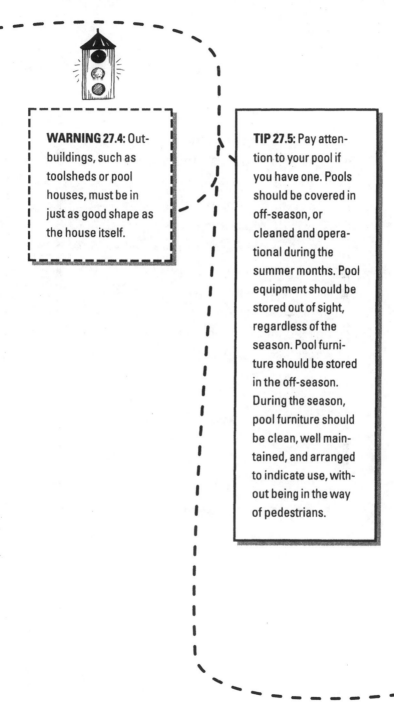

WARNING 27.4: Outbuildings, such as toolsheds or pool houses, must be in just as good shape as the house itself.

TIP 27.5: Pay attention to your pool if you have one. Pools should be covered in off-season, or cleaned and operational during the summer months. Pool equipment should be stored out of sight, regardless of the season. Pool furniture should be stored in the off-season. During the season, pool furniture should be clean, well maintained, and arranged to indicate use, without being in the way of pedestrians.

28

Pay attention to odors, ventilation, and sound. Just as appearances can turn someone off, so can foul odors and loud noises. Now is the time to address the causes of any offensive odors from the kitchen and bathrooms. Make sure to remove musty smells from basements or below ground living areas. If you wait until you're showing the house to do so, your last-ditch efforts—fans and room fresheners—will be obvious and actually call attention to the problem. Similarly, do all you can to address the causes of any offensive sounds.

☐ **Done**

TIP 28.1: To eliminate the smells of stale smoke and Fido, vacuum draperies and upholstery, and use a carpet cleaner. Cooking odors can be vanquished by using your stove's exhaust system, or purchasing an air purifier. As for the dreaded mildew, disinfect problem areas frequently, and don't let laundry pile up.

CO-OP & CONDO OWNER'S TIP 28.2: Not all of us can afford the peace and quiet of a penthouse. If your apartment is on a low floor and is subject to the sounds of the street, investigate the cost of soundproofing windows that face the street.

29 Consider making inexpensive cosmetic additions.

Now isn't the time to fix a poor floor plan, but you can do things to mitigate problem areas inside the house. For example, consider putting a light in a dark corner, or increasing the bulb wattage if it's insufficient. If sight lines are a problem in narrow, windowless areas, a strategically placed, inexpensive, framed mirror can make all the difference in the world. For more tips and ideas, see Stage 5.

☐ **Done**

30

Consider tuning up any building systems in need. You shouldn't be investing in a new boiler or new hot-water system at this point, but if your preinspection showed any deficiencies in the building systems do whatever you can, within reason, to make sure they're acceptable.

☐ **Done**

TIP 30.1: Make sure you have up-to-date files on your appliances and building systems. Include maintenance receipts, warranties and service contracts, and product literature. Being able to produce such comprehensive files could ease buyers' qualms about older appliances or systems.

TIP 30.2: Be sure your heating and cooling systems are in working order. Call in your regular maintenance people for a tune-up.

31

Address any signs of insect infestation now. If your preinspection shows any sign of termite, carpenter ant, or other damaging insect infestation, have the problem treated now, and sign up for a contract for ongoing exterminations. Few things scare a buyer more than finding insect problems. It's better to get the job taken care of now, when you have the chance to avoid scaring off a potential buyer.

☐ **Done**

WARNING 31.1: If your preinspection detects asbestos in your home—probably from insulation in your basement—you may have to foot the bill for it to be taken care of if you want to sell your home. Removal of asbestos is an incredibly complex and costly process. Instead, the asbestos can be *encapsulated,* or covered, and thereby rendered harmless. Get estimates of the cost as soon as you discover the problem, and either have it taken care of before you put the home on the market, or make the broker aware of the problem and provide written estimates for dealing with it.

WARNING 31.2: If your preinspection shows signs of radon contamination you may have a severe problem. First, have the test repeated. Then, depending on the second set of findings, find out if the problem can be treated with increased ventilation. Just as with asbestos, it's better to deal with the problem on your own if you can.

PUT TOGETHER YOUR TEAM

With your home now as unobjectionable as vanilla ice cream, the next stage in the selling process is to assemble a team of professionals—a real estate broker and an attorney—to help you sell your home as quickly and for as much money as possible. Your goal in this stage is to find and retain professionals who truly have your best interests at heart, and who are willing to work hard for their commission or fee.

32

Realize you definitely need a real estate broker. While there are many self-proclaimed real estate experts who say you're better off selling your home without a broker, I just don't agree. When buyers know you're selling on your own, they immediately cut their offers by the 6 percent you think you're saving. Therefore, there's no real savings. In addition, a good broker can serve as a valuable intermediary, a source of insight into the other side, a marketing adviser, and, if you're forced to sell off-season, a way to tap into a vanishing audience of potential buyers.

☐ **Done**

33 Find candidate brokers.
Ask your attorney and accountant for their recommendations if they live in your area. Ask your neighbors and friends if they know of a good broker. If you're friendly with the manager of a local bank, ask him or her for some names.

☐ **Done**

CO-OP & CONDO OWNER'S TIP 33.1: Ask members of your building's or development's board for the names of brokers who have successfully sold units in the development. Not only will this provide you with a broker who knows the strengths and weaknesses of your building or development, but it will also help you in prescreening buyers so you know they'll be acceptable to your board.

34

Gauge how much of a local presence each agency is. It's essential that the broker you select has experience in your particular area. Not only will that help in determining value and pricing, but it will mean they're better able to sell the home's features.

☐ **Done**

TIP 34.1: One excellent way to see how much of a local presence a brokerage firm is, is to drive around and count the number of signs they have on front lawns in a five-mile circle around your home.

TIP 34.2: Another, somewhat easier, but less certain way to check local presence is to read the ads in local newspapers. Count how many homes within a five-mile circle around your home are listed by each candidate brokerage.

35

Narrow the field. From the names you've solicited and your screening for local expertise, select three candidates who have a strong presence in your area and come highly recommended.

□ **Done**

36

Call each candidate and schedule a visit. Telephone each candidate and set up a time for them to come to your home to visit and speak with you. If at all possible, set these meetings up for daylight hours so they can see the home at its best.

☐ **Done**

TIP 36.1: When calling the agency, before you say anything else, ask to speak with the manager. In most agencies, the person who fields the call gets the listing. You want more than luck on your side. Tell the manager that his or her agency comes highly recommended by your contact and that you don't want your home simply assigned to the next person in line. Place the burden on the manager, and say you want a full-time salesperson with experience.

WARNING 36.2: Real estate selling is an easy field to enter. Far too many brokers are in the business by default, rather than design. Many are part-timers who are little more than advanced amateurs. You want a real pro who can help complete your education about the selling process. The broker must be able to serve as your Trojan horse, getting information about a potential buyer you couldn't get on your own. He or she must also be able to serve as your poker face, relaying information without revealing your ultimate goals.

TIP 36.3: The signs of a pro, other than being a full-timer with lots of experience, is a professional personal appearance and membership in the National Association of Real Estate Brokers. (If you feel the need to check on a candidate's claimed membership, the association can be reached at 202-785-4477.) For questions to ask a broker, see tip #38.1, p. 89.

37 **Conduct a silent tour of the home.** When each broker arrives at your home, give him or her a tour, but don't describe the house or try to sell them. You're interested in what they say. This is an interview—you're not selling them on the house, they should be selling you on their expertise. What they say about your house, what they see, is what they'll pass along to potential buyers. The more they notice, the better they'll be at selling your home.

☐ **Done**

WARNING 37.1: Don't be swayed by praise. You're more interested in a broker's acuity than in how much they love your home. Far too many sellers fall victim to brokers' flattery and promises of a high selling price.

TIP 37.2: If they don't say anything, ask them for their comments, and say you're eager for blunt, honest input. Some brokers may not want to offer opinions until they've been asked, for fear of insulting a sensitive seller.

38

Quiz the broker. Once the tour is completed, sit down with the broker and interview him or her.

☐ **Done**

TIP 38.1: Here are some questions to ask candidate brokers:

• How big is your agency? How many people do you have on staff?

• How long have you been employed by this agency? What was your prior experience?

• Are you a member of any professional organizations or associations?

• What is your sales experience in the neighborhood?

• In this area, what is the average length of time between placing a listing and shaking hands on a deal? (The broker's answer to this question will give you an idea of their knowledge of the market.)

• Can you give me the names and phone numbers of the sellers of the last three houses you sold in my area and price range?

TIP 38.2: All other things being equal, the bigger the brokerage the better, since more brokers on staff means more potential buyers being brought to see your home.

39

Ask for price estimates and verbal comparables. Even after a short visit, an experienced broker should be able to give you an idea of what price range your home falls into. He or she should also be able to provide some anecdotal backup for this estimate, in the form of *verbal comps*—reminiscences of recent sales of comparable homes in the area.

☐ **Done**

40

Ask for formal comps. After hearing their verbal comps, ask the broker to back up his or her ideas with documentation. This should be in the form of *written comps*—printouts of sales from the past three to six months, listing asking price, selling price, and the features and locations of the homes. Sometimes these come with photos as well.

☐ **Done**

TIP 40.1: Another way to judge the expertise of a broker is to see how closely the formal comps you are given match your home. If the descriptions of the homes are nearly identical to yours, the broker is on the ball. If they're not even close, the broker is looking to justify his or her estimate, rather than documenting an accurate opinion.

CO-OP & CONDO OWNER'S WARNING 40.2: Owners of co-ops and condos need to obtain comps from their individual building or development in order to price their home accurately. But that can be very tough for co-op owners since there are no deeds recorded on co-op transactions. That means they have to rely on brokers for the information. If there have been no sales in a building or development during the past year, use sales in nearby buildings or developments similar in character. However, they can be considered a rough guide only, because issues vary from co-op to co-op.

41 Explain the type of arrangement you're interested in.

Tell each broker that you are willing to offer the agency you choose a limited exclusive. That means they have the exclusive right to sell your home for a limited period of time. Ask what they are willing to offer you in exchange for that exclusive right. In specific, ask what kind of marketing program they can commit to, including multiple listings, open houses, advertising, and preparation of a brochure to be used in a mail campaign.

☐ **Done**

42

Select a broker. Of the three brokers you've met with, choose the one who seems the most professional and who, in your gut estimation, will best represent your interests. The best possible broker is someone who makes a good impression and who combines honesty and street smarts.

☐ **Done**

WARNING 42.1: This ISN'T the time to negotiate the broker's fees.

TIP 42.2: This IS the time to discuss logistics, such as what are the best times of day for the house to be shown, and how much warning you need before a showing.

43

Use leverage to improve your position. Having selected your top choice, approach the broker and say that you'd like to hire him or her . . . but the broker must match the best elements of the deals you've been offered from the other agencies. In almost all cases, he or she will readily agree.

☐ **Done**

44

Negotiate the terms of your listing agreement. Tell the broker you'll give his or her agency a thirty-day exclusive with three thirty-day renewals at your option. This kind of arrangement gives you the best of both worlds. It lets you stick with a broker who's doing well, and lets you leave a broker who's not, without wasting the entire selling season.

☐ **Done**

TIP 44.1: If you already have your attorney in place it's a good idea to have him or her review the brokerage agreement before you sign it. That way you won't inadvertently relinquish your rights.

WARNING 44.2: The biggest issue you want to address in the brokerage agreement is the timing of paying the broker's commission. In most states, brokers are actually entitled to their commission when they've simply produced a willing buyer. You want the document to read that payment will be made "if, as, and when" title closes.

TIP 44.3: If you must compromise to reach an agreement with the broker, agree to at most a sixty-day exclusive with two thirty-day renewals.

TIP 44.4: If you do agree to an exclusive, make sure you get something in return, such as a commitment by the broker to an advertising campaign, preparation of a brochure for a mail campaign, and at least one open house. These commitments should be made in writing as part of the brokerage agreement.

TIP 44.5: Try to include at least one exclusion to an exclusive brokerage agreement: that if you sell the home without the broker's assistance you don't have to pay the brokerage fee. There are a number of variations you can negotiate here. One is that if you personally showed the home prior to retaining the broker, and one of those parties buys, you don't have to pay. An even better option is that you are released from the obligation of paying the commission if you personally sell your home at any time throughout the process. If you must give some ground on this point, try to settle on giving them 25 percent of their commission if you sell.

TIP 44.6: Consider offering a bonus—perhaps a round-trip airline ticket to Europe—to a salesperson who sells your house within thirty days.

45 Find candidate attorneys.

While the legal work involved in the sale of a home isn't extraordinarily difficult, this isn't the time to skimp on an attorney. You want someone who is experienced and able to work quickly, because the speed with which you move from accepted offer to signed contract is essential. Once buyers commit they tend to get cold feet. You don't want to give them too much time to dwell on their fears. Ask your accountant and banker for recommendations. In addition, speak with family, friends, and co-workers who are in an economic bracket similar to yours. Your state's bar association is another source. Ask for the chairperson of the real estate committee. He or she should be able to provide the names of attorneys who regularly handle transactions similar to yours. Come up with three names.

☐ **Done**

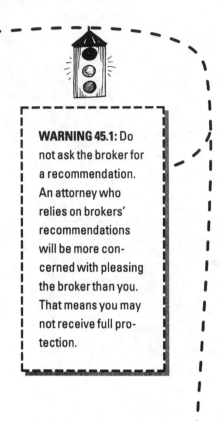

WARNING 45.1: Do not ask the broker for a recommendation. An attorney who relies on brokers' recommendations will be more concerned with pleasing the broker than you. That means you may not receive full protection.

46

Interview each candidate attorney. Call each candidate attorney and schedule a meeting at his or her office. You need to interview each one for the job.

☐ **Done**

TIP 46.1: Here are some questions you should ask every candidate attorney:

• What is the nature and length of your experience in home sales?

• What do you perceive to be the potential problems in this kind of transaction?

• Will you be delegating any work? If so, to whom, and how much will it cost?

• Do you engage in any continuing education? [To keep up with changing laws.]

• Do you charge an hourly rate or a flat fee for handling this type of transaction? [Hourly fees, depending on the experience of the lawyer and location, range from $100/hour to $300/hour. In my experience, the number of hours can range from two to ten. This presupposes professional behavior on both sides.]

• What is your flat fee?

• What is your hourly billing rate?

• How many billable hours have you found the average transaction takes?

• What is your policy on billing for transactions that are, for some reason, broken off?

• Are you available in the evening or on weekends?

TIP 46.2: Be certain you explain to the attorney that you want to be able to have a contract ready within forty-eight hours of an accepted offer, and that you'd like to have a sit-down meeting to hammer out the contract. You need your lawyer to act quickly in order to minimize buyer's cold feet.

WARNING 46.3: Any attorney who refuses to meet with you prior to being engaged, or who wants to charge you for this meeting, should be scratched from your list of candidates.

WARNING 46.4: An attorney who takes multiple telephone calls while you are interviewing him or her is a highly questionable candidate.

WARNING 46.5: An attorney who barks at his or her staff, while being sweet to you, may lose the sugar coating once hired.

TIP 46.6: Pay attention to the attorney's desk. It's a sign of his or her organizational skills and ability to handle matters efficiently.

TIP 46.7: All things being equal, opt for the attorney with the most real estate experience, even if that means paying a bit more. If things move smoothly, the number of hours you'll be billed for will be less with an experienced pro. And if things don't go smoothly, you want someone on your team who has seen it all before and isn't surprised by anything that happens.

WARNING 46.8: The residential real estate process is different from state to state. Some have systems in place in which brokers prepare the contracts—using boilerplate forms— and title companies handle closings. Regardless of the custom or practice in your area, and despite brokers' warnings that lawyers can be impediments to making deals, I urge you to hire your own attorney and get him or her actively involved in the process. Otherwise, there's no professional involved in the transaction who represents your best interests.

47

Select an attorney and have him or her sign an engagement letter. After interviewing your candidates, select the one with whom you're most comfortable to represent your legal interests. Seal the deal by signing an engagement letter that spells out the obligations and responsibilities of both parties, all fees, and any other relevant details.

☐ **Done**

TIP 47.1: Here's a sample engagement letter:

John Q. Seller
10 Maple Street
Anytown, USA

Date

Attorney & Counsel, Esquires
5 Courthouse Lane
Anytown, USA

Re: Sale of House/10 Maple Street, Anytown, USA

Dear Mr. Counsel:

Thank you for agreeing to act as my attorney in connection with the sale of my home. You have agreed to devote sufficient time and attention to this matter consistent with my desire to sell my home in the time frame we have discussed (or insert date). Specifically, you have agreed to prepare and deliver a Contract of Sale to the buyer's attorney within forty-eight hours from the time I advise you of an accepted offer. You agree to return all telephone calls promptly, and to keep me apprised of all relevant matters. In addition, you agree to furnish me with a closing memo and closing statement, together with original documents and copies of all checks.

In consideration of your services I will be charged a flat, fixed fee of $_____, plus out-of-pocket expenses—at your firm's actual cost—for photocopying, facsimile, overnight mail, and messenger services. The latter two expenses are only to be incurred when absolutely necessary.

(If an hourly rate is negotiated, agree upon a cap so you can be sure the fee will not exceed a certain amount. Also, specify rates of all staff who will be working on the file—and state that paralegals and lower-billing associates will be utilized whenever possible and appropriate.)

I may terminate our relationship at any time and for any reason, whereupon I will pay your fee up to the point of termination—unless the amount is disputed—and you agree to return my entire file to me immediately. In the event a dispute arises with respect to our financial arrangement which we are unable to resolve in good faith, we agree to submit the dispute for final and binding arbitration before the closest office of the American Arbitration Association.

I look forward to a mutually beneficial relationship.

AGREED TO: Very truly yours,

_____   _____
Real T. Counsel, Esq.   John Q. Seller

FIND THE RIGHT PRICE RANGE

With your professional team in place, the next stage in the home-selling process is to find out in which price range your home falls. This will require some digging, some thought, and some objective analysis, but in the long run your efforts will pay off with a speedy sale. The goal is to pin your home's value down to a range of plus or minus 15 percent.

48

Start studying the formal comps you were given. Go through each of the formal comps you were given by the candidate real estate brokers and recheck their validity. Take the most accurate comps (approximately the same square footage, same number of rooms, same neighborhood) and divide them into two categories: those sold within the past three months, and those sold earlier.

☐ **Done**

49 **Try to determine a value range based on the most recent comps.** Take the most recent comps and list their selling prices on a sheet of paper. Then, rewrite them as a range from lowest to highest. For example: from $142,000 to $150,000.

☐ **Done**

TIP 49.1: Real estate values are subjective since they're somewhat based on personal taste. As a rule they can best be expressed as a range of about 10 percent. For example: $200,000 to $220,000; or $150,000 to $165,000. If the range you come up with from studying the formal comps falls into this 10 percent pattern, you've probably got an accurate gauge of your home's value.

CO-OP & CONDO OWNER'S WARNING 49.2: Co-op and condo owners must become know-it-alls about their building's or development's financial status in order to price their home correctly. With co-ops, poor building finances or sky-high maintenance costs must be compensated for with a lower asking price. With condos, overblown real estate taxes and/or high common charges often force similar pricing concessions.

50

Double-check the validity of your comps. Before you accept the range you've come up with as etched in stone, take a look at as many of the comps as you can. While you won't be able to go inside, you should be able to make a fairly accurate estimate as to whether or not they're comparable to your own home's size, condition, location, and character.

☐ **Done**

TIP 50.1: If you're not secure with this kind of market testing for value, get a recommendation from your banker for a real estate appraiser. Having a formal appraisal done shouldn't cost more than $250 to $500, depending on your area. And if you're home is worth, say, more than $300,000, it's definitely worth getting.

WARNING 50.2: An appraisal is, at best, based on prior sales that do not necessarily indicate the present value, which may be higher or lower. The offerings you receive from the broker should establish that trend.

51

Try to get a sense of market trends. Repeat the process of going through the comps and coming up with a value range, but this time use the comps that are more than three months old. This can give you a sense as to whether values are holding steady, increasing, or decreasing. Run your findings by your broker to see if they are accurate. Obviously, if values are decreasing, speed is even more important. The number of days a home was on the market before sale indicates whether the market is very active, moderately active, slow, or very slow.

☐ **Done**

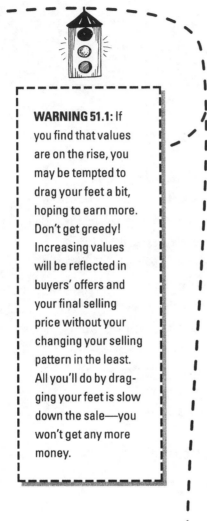

WARNING 51.1: If you find that values are on the rise, you may be tempted to drag your feet a bit, hoping to earn more. Don't get greedy! Increasing values will be reflected in buyers' offers and your final selling price without your changing your selling pattern in the least. All you'll do by dragging your feet is slow down the sale—you won't get any more money.

52 **Verify your findings with your broker.** After coming up with a value range for your home, run your findings by the broker once again. Specifically ask if there's anything he or she can think of that would place your home at either the high or low end of the range, or in another range entirely.

☐ **Done**

SET YOUR PRICE AND MARKET YOUR PRODUCT

Having found out about how much your home is worth in the prior stage, it's now time to put a specific number on its price tag. This decision, as you'll see, is more of a marketing decision than a financial one. Having done that, you'll next turn to the heart of this book— the marketing of your home. The goal of this stage is to make your house as attractive as possible to potential buyers in order to obtain as high a price for it as you can.

53 **Realize that the price you set is part of your marketing.** Picking a price for your home from within the range you've determined to be its value is a function of marketing more than anything else. You must accept that nothing you do can increase the price you get for your home beyond the range of its value. Accepting this, more than anything else, will help you sell your home quickly.

☐ **Done**

54

Recognize that the selling price will be below your asking price. Real estate is one of the few areas in American commerce where buyers believe they have a right to negotiate. In fact, negotiation is such an ingrained part of the process that they will automatically assume you have priced your home above its value, and above what you're willing to accept, in order to have room for negotiation.

☐ **Done**

TIP 54.1: In America, the average gap between the price a home is put on the market for and what it is sold for is 6 or 7 percent. That assumes, of course, that it's neither a buyer's nor a seller's market. Obviously, in a seller's market the gap is smaller, and in a buyer's market the gap is larger.

55

Recognize that there are market ranges that you must be aware of. You already know that there are price ranges for homes, generally around 10 percent. There are also buyer's ranges. These represent the range of variously priced homes that particular buyers will look at. For homes priced under $500,000 there are eight buyer's ranges:

under $100,000;
$100,000 to $150,000;
$150,000 to $200,000;
$200,000 to $250,000;
$250,000 to $300,000;
$300,000 to $350,000;
$350,000 to $400,000; and
$400,000 to $500,000.

☐ **Done**

56 Resolve that you will not allow your home to fall into the wrong buyer's range.

Let's say your home's value range is between $135,000 and $150,000. Knowing that homes are initially listed at a higher price than they sell for, you might be tempted to list your home for more than $150,000. If you do that, however, you'll be dealing with the wrong group of potential buyers: those looking for homes in the $150,000 to $200,000 range. Your home will not look good in comparison to everything else they're seeing. You want buyers whose range is $100,000 to $150,000 instead.

☐ **Done**

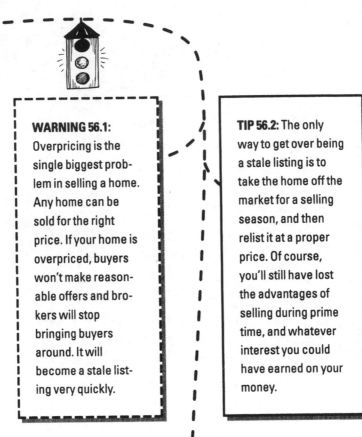

WARNING 56.1: Overpricing is the single biggest problem in selling a home. Any home can be sold for the right price. If your home is overpriced, buyers won't make reasonable offers and brokers will stop bringing buyers around. It will become a stale listing very quickly.

TIP 56.2: The only way to get over being a stale listing is to take the home off the market for a selling season, and then relist it at a proper price. Of course, you'll still have lost the advantages of selling during prime time, and whatever interest you could have earned on your money.

57 Decide whether your home falls in the top, middle, or bottom of its range value.

Having sworn off pricing your home outside the appropriate buyer's range, return your focus to its value range. After looking at your comps and other homes on the market, objectively decide if your home falls at the top, middle, or bottom of that range. Going back to the example of a home in the $135,000 to $150,000 range, does yours most resemble homes that have sold for $135,000, $142,000, or $147,000?

☐ **Done**

58

Select a price based on where your home falls within the value range. If your home falls at the top of the $135,000 to $150,000 range, consider pricing it at $149,500. That's clearly in the right buyer's range, but it's also clearly at the top of the value range. If your home falls in the middle of the same range, consider pricing it at $145,500. That shows an objective appreciation of its actual value. If your home falls in the low end of the range, consider $139,500. Again, that shows you're a serious seller.

☐ **Done**

TIP 58.1: Far too many sellers price their homes too high initially and are forced to come down a great deal in the negotiations. It's better to price your home more accurately initially—thereby attracting more potential buyers— and be less generous during negotiations. (See Stage 6.)

TIP 58.2: For whatever reason, odd prices, like $149,500, seem to be perceived as being more seriously thought out than even prices, like $150,000.

TIP 58.3: Tacking on an extra $500 to your price—$149,500 rather than just $149,000—won't lose you any potential buyers, yet offers you a little bit more room to negotiate.

TIP 58.4: If you're selling in a very brisk market, or your home is in a very desirable area, consider edging your home up from the middle of the range to the top end, or from the low end to the middle. Do not, however, get greedy and try to move your home from the top end of one buyer's range to the bottom of another. It will come back to haunt you.

59

Define your listing. Having picked a price, sit down with your broker and go over exactly what should be included in the description of the home, which is called the listing. Obviously, any personal property, such as air conditioners, refrigerators, or light fixtures that will be included in the sale should be mentioned. In addition, state when occupancy would be available. If there's a possibility of speeding up occupancy—for the right price—add that as well.

☐ **Done**

TIP 59.1: Think about leaving one or two potentially desirable items of personal property out of the listing; for instance, a chandelier in the dining room or the new side-by-side refrigerator/freezer. Doing so will give you more room to negotiate later on. Rather than making a price concession, you can offer to include one of these previously excluded items.

TIP 59.2: If you have architect's plans for a proposed extension, consider including their availability in the listing.

CO-OP & CONDO OWNER'S TIP 59.3: Remember you're not just selling a home, you're selling a lifestyle. Your listing (as well as your buyer's booklet—see Step 61, p. 131) should include information about the special amenities offered in your building or development. Include information on health clubs, laundry facilities, concierge services, as well as building maintenance and security. Data on building or development associations or organizations may be important as well.

60

Contact your attorney. In order to make sure your attorney will be able to provide a draft contract quickly, pass along a copy of your listing. That way, the items included and excluded can be inserted into the agreement.

☐ **Done**

WARNING 60.1: Make sure your attorney has all the information he or she needs. Your attorney should ask you for a copy of your deed to determine in whose name(s) title to the house is held and what the form of ownership is. The legal description put on the contract and new deed must match the old deed or transfer of title could be impeded. He or she should also ask you for a copy of your title insurance policy and a property survey.

61

Create a buyer's booklet. This is a handout describing your home that those visiting it can take away with them. It gets very confusing looking at house after house. Buyers often forget exactly what they saw where, and few bother to take notes or photos. The contents of this handout are limited only by your imagination. Have 100 copies of your booklet made up.

☐ **Done**

TIP 61.1: If your utility bills are unusually low, either because of a very efficient heating and cooling system or superb insulation, consider including copies of them, particularly the page comparing your usage to the area average. If your house uses well water, consider including a copy of the positive report on its water quality.

TIP 61.2: If there are any interior or exterior flaws in the design of your home, you may want to consider including suggested renovation plans in with your buyer's booklet. For instance, if yours is an old home with a separate shower room and toilet room, a proposed plan for combining the two into a traditional bathroom could make the difference between getting an offer or not. It's certainly a lot cheaper than having the actual work done, and buyers will appreciate your being open about something they're bound to notice anyway.

TIP 61.3: Include photos showing your home during other seasons, especially if you're selling in the fall or winter. Even if you're selling in prime time, a heartwarming winter photo featuring a wreath on the front door can be a boon as well.

TIP 61.4: Consider including nighttime photos of your floodlight systems. Floodlighting can enhance your property, but buyers won't know what it has done for yours because they'll be viewing your home during the day. To make sure they're aware of just how impressive and secure your home can appear at night, include a couple of photos in the buyer's booklet. Make sure the pictures are taken with fast, available-light color film.

TIP 61.5: Include a floor plan in the booklet. Buyers often see several houses in the space of one day. By giving them a floor plan you virtually guarantee yours won't get lost in the shuffle. A rough layout of the rooms on each floor drawn on grid paper, noting the approximate measurement, will do.

TIP 61.6: Buyers are going to want to know all the costs involved in owning your home. Include the information in your booklet. List real estate tax information, water fees, garbage collection fees, etc. If appliances are to be included in the sale of your home, note their model numbers.

TIP 61.7: Consider including a map of your area in the buyer's booklet. You might know that the dry cleaner and local convenience store are a mere five minutes away, but don't assume buyers do. Either procure a town map through the local chamber of commerce and make copies for your handout, or else make your own simplified map of the area. In either case, mark the location of stores, schools, the hospital, the post office, gas stations, libraries, churches, parks, laundromats, and restaurants.

TIP 61.8: Include a description of the schools in your area, obviously highlighting their positive traits and offering up any impressive statistics. This information should be easily attainable by calling the school board. If buyers have children, the quality of the school district will be very important to them.

TIP 61.9: If your home was built before 1900, consider including a history of the house. Buyers are likely to be charmed by a home with a story or pedigree attached to it. You can usually obtain the name and background of the original owner from deeds filed with the town clerk. By the way, prior ownership by clergy, as well as by someone famous or infamous, is considered a positive factor.

CO-OP & CONDO OWNER'S TIP 61.10: Don't let a less-than-perfect view detract from your home's selling potential. Rather than letting buyers consider it a negative, take the issue on directly by adding a line to your booklet such as "typical city view."

62

Resolve to make yourself scarce. Nothing inhibits both a broker and a buyer more than having the seller hovering around. The presence of the seller can keep buyers from speaking freely, lingering, or examining the home closely.

☐ **Done**

TIP 62.1: If you can't leave the house, go to a room that's out of the main flow, making yourself as inconspicuous as possible.

TIP 62.2: Make your pets scarce as well. That means taking Fido with you when you leave. And that includes any caged reptiles or birds. At best they'll divert the buyer's attention from selling features. At worst buyers will be turned off. You might even consider sending pets to "summer camp" during the selling season. Tropical fish can stay, however—just make sure to remove any that die.

TIP 62.3: If you must stick around, show extra consideration for the buyer by providing refreshments. Coffee will warm the bones—and hearts—of even the weariest winter house hunter, just as refreshing lemonade will make summer home viewing more pleasant. Just be sure to make yourself scarce after serving. Don't offer ashtrays, however. You don't want the house reeking of tobacco for the next shopper—who will probably be someone who's highly allergic to cigarette smoke.

63 Be willing to show your home at the drop of a hat.

This means your house should be available for viewing when it's most convenient for buyers, not when it's most convenient for you. If you work during the day, make sure the agent has a key so he or she can show your home from nine to five. The same should hold true if you're planning to leave town—there's no reason why your home can't be shown while you're away. Exercise common sense, however: Don't leave valuable jewels or cash lying around.

☐ **Done**

TIP 63.1: Involve the whole family in last minute cleanups. If an agent calls and says he or she will be coming by with buyers in twenty minutes, there's no reason for you to go into cardiac arrest and rush around trying to tidy things up on your own. Instead, get everyone in the family to pitch in, whether that means putting toys away or loading last night's dishes into the dishwasher. Accept that there's no way the house is going to look perfect. Do the best you can, and then let it go when the doorbell rings. NEVER apologize about the condition of your home. It starts things out on the wrong foot. And DON'T throw all your junk into one room and lock the door. All rooms must be unlocked and accessible.

64 **Let the world know your house is for sale.** Word of mouth can be a powerful selling tool, and it won't cost you a cent. Put a sign out front as well . . . even if your town or neighbors frown upon it.

☐ **Done**

65

Prepare the house for company. An essential but often overlooked part of marketing a home is making it look special. You'll already have cleaned and repaired it. Now you're dressing it up to look its best. Your goal should be making it look like either a model home, or a house that's ready for a festive dinner party.

☐ **Done**

TIP 65.1: Pay attention to the local weather report and try to schedule viewings of your home when you know it's going to be sunny. It can have a tremendous effect on buyers' attitudes.

TIP 65.2: If there are any potentially objectionable noises in the area—busy streets, barking dogs next door—consider having subtle music playing all the time. There are also tapes you can buy that contain soothing sounds, like the sound of waves lapping the shore.

TIP 65.3: If you opt to have music playing in the background while your home is viewed, consider your selection. Different music is likely to appeal to different buyers. For example, if you think your home would be most attractive to first-time buyers, play light classical music, or contemporary rock or jazz. If you're aiming for trade-up buyers, play subtle, sophisticated instrumental music— Bach, Mozart, Vivaldi, or something New Age. If you'll probably be selling to empty nesters who are buying down, play things like Sinatra, Tony Bennett, or instrumental music from the forties, fifties, and sixties.

TIP 65.4: Turn on all lights before buyers arrive. This includes lights in closets, basements, and attics.

TIP 65.5: Let some fresh air in before showing your home. This means opening the window in every room for a short period before buyers arrive, even if it's only for a few minutes. Air-conditioned homes are not exempt: air them out to do away with any lingering pet or food odors you might be oblivious to. If weather permits, leave windows open while showing your home.

TIP 65.6: Whether your home is one year old or one hundred years old, it will sell quicker if it smells like new. This is best achieved by: having the painting done as close as possible to the time you're showing the house; polishing furniture with lemon-scented oils or sprays; and touching up wooden floors and cabinets with either polyurethane or Val-Oil. Both of these produce that mild, petroleum-based smell people associate with newness. Val-Oil is particularly effective, and can be found at most hardware stores.

WARNING 65.7: Don't be cheap with the heat or air-conditioning. Buyers want to feel comfortable as they walk through your home. A cold house will make buyers wonder if the furnace is about to give up the ghost, and a hot house will make them feel so uncomfortable all they'll be able to think about is leaving. Remember that it's to your advantage to make the climate of your home as pleasant as possible.

WARNING 65.8: Home buyers are nosy—they are going to open every closet, every cabinet, and even the refrigerator. Make sure closets and cabinets aren't so tightly packed that something could fall out when the door is opened. And check that there is nothing offensive-looking or foul-smelling in the refrigerator or freezer.

66

Let in as much sun as possible. Keep shades rolled up, Venetian blinds open, and get rid of heavy draperies. Make sure light isn't being cut off by overgrown foliage by checking on trees and shrubs outside first-floor windows. A light home is a warm home, and a warm home will sell for more.

☐ **Done**

TIP 66.1: If weather permits, keep the front door open. This tells the buyer yours is a welcoming home, one which you're comfortable having anyone enter. It signals just as strongly that you have nothing to hide and that your neighborhood is absolutely safe.

TIP 66.2: Remove hanging plants from windows. This will allow twice the amount of light in.

WARNING 66.3: Closed curtains or drapes make buyers wonder what there is outside that you don't want them to see. If you're trying to disguise an unsightly view, go for sheer white panels that will let in light while at the same time covering the window. Or price interior window shutters—the louvers will allow you to control the amount of light coming in while hiding the neighbor's clothesline from view.

67

Accessorize, accessorize, accessorize. We're not talking about filling up rooms with so many knickknacks it looks like a museum. What you're aiming for is adding personal touches that make a room comfortable, not cluttered: a well-placed vase of flowers, an open book on an antique desk. Go through each room of the house deciding what enhances (a strategically placed pillow) and what detracts (a picture of your mother in the hospital).

☐ **Done**

WARNING 67.1: Remove offending items and keep them well out of sight until your home is sold. That means *Playboy* magazine shouldn't be left on the coffee table, and hunting rifles shouldn't be on display in the living room. Even zany refrigerator magnets are a no-no.

TIP 67.2: Draw attention to your home's best selling features by using color and light. Bold patterns and colors draw immediate attention, but beware of going overboard—you don't want to blind anyone. Spotlighting can be used to create ambiance or highlight outstanding architectural details. Experiment.

TIP 67.3: Make sure each room has a focal point, whether it's a fireplace or a furnishing such as a painting or a unique piece of furniture. If you can, try to place the focal point as far from the entry to the room as possible. This will help stretch the surrounding area and enhance visual impact.

TIP 67.4: Capitalize on cathedral ceilings and exposed beams. These are definite selling points—if you can get buyers to look up and notice them. To draw attention to beams, hang plants, dried flowers, copper pots—whatever goes best with your decor. Cathedral ceilings can be enhanced with well-directed lighting. Be creative.

TIP 67.5: Trim and moldings add character to a room, whether applied to walls, ceilings, or even doors. They are relatively inexpensive to add or upgrade. You can get them precut from a lumberyard or home improvement center.

TIP 67.6: Add a touch of color to the outside of the house. You want your house to appear unique and special. This can be easily achieved by placing a pot of flowers on the front step. Consider adding a nice welcome mat and perhaps wind chimes there as well. Just make sure the wind isn't too strong—subtlety is the key.

TIP 67.7: Fresh flowers on the dining room table and in a few other select locations—the hall table, a bedroom—not only add a lovely scent, but also convey class and cleanliness. If they come from your own garden that's even better.

TIP 67.8: If the fresh flowers don't come from your own garden you could imply they do—and that you pay a great deal of attention to the grounds—by leaving an attractive, hardcover book on gardening open on a nightstand.

68

Let your entry hall do the talking. You need to grab a buyer's attention the minute he or she steps in the house, and nothing does this better than a strategically placed vase of flowers or piece of artwork. Other entry-hall accents that can be helpful are coatracks and umbrella stands.

☐ **Done**

TIP 68.1: If you lack an entry hall, create one. No one likes to walk directly into a living room. Create a partial partition by using a bookcase or a narrow table with flowers on it. The idea is to make the potential buyer feel as if he or she has stepped into a separate entry hall while still having access to your living room.

TIP 68.2: Another way to create the illusion of separateness is through the use of lighting. Almost anything will do— sconces, a lamp on a table—just as long as it differs from the light being used in the living room.

69

Convey coziness in living rooms and/or family rooms.
A quilt draped over the arm of a couch, a set of checkers on the coffee table, a well-placed musical instrument resting in a corner—all these tell buyers that an active and happy family life takes place in these rooms, a life you want them to be able to imagine should they buy your home.

☐ **Done**

WARNING 69.1: Cozy doesn't mean sloppy, however. Steer clear of creating a look that's too lived-in.

TIP 69.2: If you've got a fireplace, use it. Have a warm, crackling fire going whenever your house is being shown. If the weather is too warm for a fire, draw attention to the fireplace by making sure the mantel features a few well-placed knickknacks and photos. Fireplace fans and well-polished brass fixtures are eye-catchers as well. Or, you could use a large-size Duraflame log alone so you've fire, but little actual heat.

TIP 69.3: Kill your TV—or at the very least, downplay its dominance in the room by pushing it into a corner, if possible. If your set is part of an entertainment center that features cabinet doors, by all means close them. TVs that double as tabletops can be problematic as well; if the top of your set is littered with magazines and/or memorabilia, clear it away pronto.

70 **Sell your dining room by setting the table.** This will stimulate a buyer's imagination and make it possible for them to imagine entertaining in this area. If your house is being shown in the morning, set the table as if for a brunch. Be sure to use colorful napkins and place settings, and spring for some wildflowers to place at the center of the table. If your house is being shown in the afternoon, set the table as if for dinner, but avoid being too formal. Use everyday dishes, not the ones you dig out once a year at the holidays.

☐ **Done**

TIP 70.1: If you normally eat meals in the kitchen, set the dining room table as if you were going to have a holiday meal. Sure it's an obvious gimmick, but it will get buyers to focus on how lovely the room will look when they're having Thanksgiving in it next year.

TIP 70.2: If your dining room is large, create the illusion of having two rooms in one. Wasted space turns buyers off; well-used space fires their imagination. There's no reason this room should be used just for dining; if space permits, turn part of it into a library by adding a chair and a reading light. The possibilities are endless.

TIP 70.3: If your dining room is small, remove excess leaves from the dining room table as well as any extra chairs, and try placing the table against the wall rather than in the center of the room. Your goal is for buyers to be able to walk through the area freely.

Make sure your kitchen conveys warmth. This is easily achieved by opening a cookbook on the counter, putting some colorful fruit in a bowl, or displaying some vegetables ready to be cut on a cutting board. Food can be extremely evocative as well: a jar of cookies or a strategically placed cake can do wonders when it comes to buyers' psyches. Last but not least, don't forget the importance of smell: A simmering potpourri can aid in conjuring up nostalgic feelings, as can a loaf of freshly baked bread. Another way to appeal to the senses is to brew a pot of coffee before buyers arrive. Is there any better smell in the world?

☐ **Done**

TIP 71.1: Capitalize on large kitchen windows by growing herbs or flowers on the sill, or hanging a mobile or wind chimes to draw a buyer's attention. Bird feeders outside the window can enhance as well, as kitchen and nature seem to blend into one.

TIP 71.2: If you have an eat-in kitchen, accentuate the cozy, breakfast-nook feel to it by setting the table for an informal meal or placing a bowl of fruit in the center of the table. Do anything you can to suggest that this is a comfy place to linger.

72 Don't forget the stairs.

Make your stairwell appealing to the eye by hanging pictures along the wall. Create a focal point on the landing by hanging an interesting piece of artwork or placing a plant in a plant stand.

☐ **Done**

73

Create a suite effect in your bedrooms. Large bedrooms are one of the most desirable features in a home. Make sure yours look as large as possible by streamlining clutter, and by creating the impression that the rooms can be used for more than sleeping: a desk, a piece of exercise equipment, or even a reading chair beside a lamp may help.

☐ **Done**

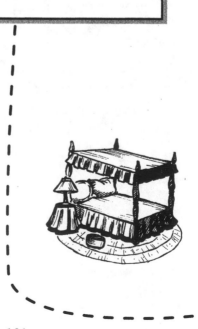

TIP 73.1: A private bathroom off the master bedroom is a bonus as well: make sure it's decorated to match or compliment the color scheme of the bedroom, and always remember to leave the bathroom door open when showing your home since some buyers feel uncomfortable opening up doors in other people's homes.

WARNING 73.2: Teens' bedrooms can torpedo the sale of your home. Though they won't be happy about it, ask yours to keep their rooms clean and impress upon them the need for a neutral look. Assure your son that he can hang his Pearl Jam poster when you move into your new home, but for now it needs to be taken down so buyers can imagine the room as more than a shrine to MTV.

74

Personalize your bathrooms.
You already know they need to be spanking clean; what you may not have realized is that like every other room in the house, bathrooms can benefit from small personal touches as well. Hang pictures; choose accessories that compliment the color of the room; and always, *always* put out fresh towels and soap. I'll assume you've already sprung for a new shower curtain and maybe even a new wooden toilet seat.

☐ **Done**

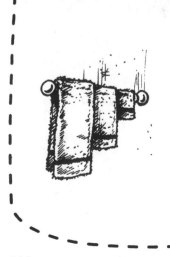

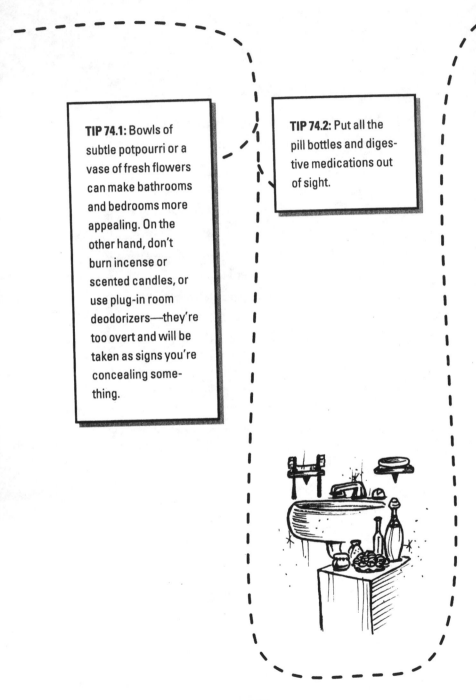

TIP 74.1: Bowls of subtle potpourri or a vase of fresh flowers can make bathrooms and bedrooms more appealing. On the other hand, don't burn incense or scented candles, or use plug-in room deodorizers—they're too overt and will be taken as signs you're concealing something.

TIP 74.2: Put all the pill bottles and digestive medications out of sight.

75

Don't forget utility rooms. Make sure your laundry room is as visually appealing and tidy as the rest of the house. This means fresh paint on the walls, dirty clothing in hampers, and clean clothes folded neatly in piles or hung on hangers. If space allows, demonstrate that the room could be used for more than one activity: laundry and sewing, for example, by placing a sewing machine in the corner.

☐ **Done**

76

Brighten your yard with flowers. This doesn't mean you suddenly have to turn into a gardener. All you need to do is go to the nursery and buy some flowering plants in baskets, or some packs of blooming annuals to be planted in tight clumps, and that should do the trick. Just make sure you do it early enough in the season so everything is in bloom when your home is being shown.

☐ **Done**

TIP 76.1: Use plants to help maximize the sales potential of a screened-in porch or deck. A few well-placed pots of geraniums can enhance deck steps, adding a touch of color. Similarly, lush plants hung from porch eaves add a personal romantic touch. Treat these areas as the treasures they are: that means no cast-off furniture or junk.

TIP 76.2: Majestic trees are natural attention-grabbers. If you have one on your property, use it: hang a swing from a sturdy branch, plant flowers around the trunk, or set up a few chairs and a table beneath the leafy boughs to convey this is a wonderfully cool, shady place to pass the time on a hot summer day.

TIP 76.3: Flat doesn't have to mean boring. If you're blessed with a yard that's level, demonstrate its uses by setting up a volleyball net or digging out your old croquet set. Any prop will do, as long as buyers get the idea that this is space that's used, not wasted.

TIP 76.4: Establish a backyard living/dining area. If your home doesn't have a deck or patio, don't worry about it: all you have to do is set up a picnic table in close proximity to an outdoor grill and they'll get the idea. Make sure the table is appealing to the eye by using a brightly colored tablecloth and plastic dishes.

77

Tell your broker you want offers in writing. The last step in this stage is to inform your broker that you would like all offers made in writing. The potential buyer's signature on such a document indicates a psychological commitment on their part to buy. In some locales, an offer is made by having the purchaser sign what amounts to a contract of sale. While these are generally the starting points for oral negotiations, once terms are reached they often help the balance of the process—contract and closing—move more swiftly.

☐ **Done**

TIP 77.1: Ask for a weekly progress report from your broker. You have a right to be kept informed, and a good agent will report back to you on buyers' reactions to your home, both positive and negative. Listen to whatever he or she says with an open mind, and see if you can correct any mistakes mentioned. Arrange to meet with your agent on an occasional basis to go over selling strategies. Be flexible, but most of all, be involved: Selling your home should be a joint effort.

NEGOTIATE THE SALE

All your marketing efforts in the prior stage have paid off and you have an offer on the table. The next stage in the process is to negotiate the final selling price. More than in any other part of the process, this is where the majority of home sellers lose their nerve, and as a result, quite a few dollars. Your goal in this stage is to end up with a selling price as close to your initial asking price as possible.

78

Quiz the broker about the potential buyer. The more you know about your buyer, the more well-positioned you are to respond to an offer. The best source of inside information is the broker.

☐ **Done**

TIP 78.1: Here are some questions about the buyer that you should ask the broker:
• Where are they from?
• How old are they?
• What do they do for a living?
• Do they have children? How many? What are their ages?
• Are they currently renters or do they own a home?
• Will they have to sell their own home before they can buy mine?
• Why are they moving?
• What are their plans for financing the purchase?
• How soon can they close?

CO-OP & CONDO OWNER'S TIP 78.2: Now is the time to have your broker—who hopefully has previous experiences with your building or development—prescreen the buyer's acceptability to the board of directors. A buyer's ability to meet the requirements of a board is, in the sale of a co-op or condo, just as important as his or her ability to get a mortgage.

79

Categorize the offer. In general there are three kinds of offers: close, workable, and ridiculous. Close offers are just that, close to where you're willing to settle. They're probably around 10 percent less than your asking price. Workable offers, while lower than you'd like, are those that you may be able to negotiate into an acceptable price. Ridiculous offers are those that show the potential buyer either has no idea what the home is worth, or is trying to make a killing. Anything below the bottom of your home's 10 percent value range indicates bottom fishing.

☐ **Done**

WARNING 79.1: Don't blame the broker for a ridiculous offer. Brokers are bound to present you with every offer, whether they think it's ridiculous or not. However, if they present an absurdly low offer without also telling you that they're doing so because they're ethically bound to, feel free to have a word with them. Some brokers will bring you an offer that's ridiculous and not comment about it, simply to show you that they're doing something.

80

Respond to ridiculous offers, but not with a reduction. Every offer, no matter how absurd, should be met with a response. You never know if the wise guy or gal who lowballed initially might not become a serious buyer after being cut down to size. However, don't respond to ridiculous offers by lowering your price, even by one dollar. Instead, respond verbally by saying that you're willing to negotiate, but only in response to serious offers.

☐ **Done**

TIP 80.1: Make sure to always use the broker or your attorney to convey your responses. You want to have a middleman you can blame if negotiations break down.

81 Respond to other offers with a significant first reduction.

When a buyer makes an offer on a home, he or she hasn't emotionally committed to it yet. Your preparation, your price, and your marketing have served as the lure. The buyer is interested, and shows that by making a serious offer. However, he or she isn't hooked yet. To do that, you need to make a significant first reduction. That will convince the buyer the home is obtainable. He or she will start picturing himself in it. Suddenly, the buyer shifts from trying to win the home, to trying not to lose the home he or she thinks has already been won.

☐ **Done**

TIP 81.1: You're going to be practicing a negotiating strategy called diminishing concessions. In other words, each reduction you make will be smaller than the previous one. This does two things: it serves to hook the buyer right away, and shows there's a limit to how far you will go.

TIP 81.2: How much of a reduction you make depends on how long you're willing to negotiate. I would suggest a drop of 1–2 percent of the asking price.

WARNING 81.3: Never tell the broker exactly how much you're willing to settle for. He or she, while paid by you, truly works for the deal. That's the only time a commission is earned. Knowing how much you're willing to accept could lead a broker to drop hints, or even just tell a buyer how much they can get the house for.

82

Carefully read the potential buyer's next offer. The response of a potential buyer to your first price reduction is called by some in the real estate industry "the great unzipping." That's because, unless the buyer is very sophisticated, this offer exposes his or her goals. It's customary in America to think negotiating means splitting the difference. Therefore potential buyer's second offers are almost always based on their willingness to settle at the midpoint between that offer and your previous concession.

☐ **Done**

TIP 82.1: Here's how it works. Let's say your house is on the market for $149,500. The buyer makes an initial offer of $141,000. You respond by lowering your price to $148,000. If the buyer comes back with $142,500, it means he's willing to settle at the midpoint between $148,000 and $142,500, or $145,000.

83

Don't settle for splitting the difference. Having made a second offer, the buyer now fully expects you to propose settling at the midpoint. Instead, make a much smaller concession, indicating that you want to settle above the midpoint. The buyer is already hooked. Having expressed a willingness to spend a considerable amount of money, the buyer isn't likely to want to lose a house they consider their own over a couple of thousand dollars.

☐ **Done**

TIP 83.1: Let's go back to the earlier example. Instead of proposing an agreement at $145,500, simply drop your price to $147,000.

84

Be prepared to resist settlement pressure. At this point, it's likely either the buyer or the broker will push for settlement at that midpoint discussed earlier. Expect the buyer to come back with an offer very close to that number, if not exactly at it. And be prepared for it to be accompanied by a bit of anger, maybe even the phrase "final offer" or "best offer." Don't succumb. There's no such thing as a final offer that's really final.

☐ **Done**

85

Make another concession. To indicate your willingness to continue negotiating, drop your price once again. But make sure it's by a smaller amount than before. This also shows the buyer that you're reaching your limit.

☐ **Done**

TIP 85.1: In our example, the appropriate response to a buyer's offer of, let's say, $145,000, would be to drop your price again, but to $146,500.

TIP 85.2: If you're having trouble getting the potential buyer to come up in price, consider adding an element of competition into the picture. Since you retained the right to sell on your own, you can explain to the broker that you're getting tired of this potential buyer's reluctance . . . especially since your cousin Fred showed the house to his brother-in-law, who's about to make an offer. This threatens the broker since he or she won't get a commission if you provide the buyer, and will lead him or her to pass the word on to the potential buyer that there's another offer. Once there's competition for something it becomes more desirable.

86 Be prepared to accept.
Your use of decreasing incre-
ments should now be clear to
both buyer and broker. It should also be
clear that you're looking for a price of at
least $146,000. If that's what the buyer
comes back with, accept it.

☐ **Done**

TIP 86.1: If you find your tough negotiating has
antagonized the other side, you can resurrect the
deal by calling the buyer directly and blaming the
problems on either your attorney or the broker.
Neither will have a problem with being used in this
manner if it keeps the deal alive.

WARNING 86.2:
Demand that even though there is an offer on the table, the brokers continue to show the property. Odds are the action will slow down dramatically, and most of the visitors will be there for comparison shopping purposes, but hold the brokers to the letter of their agreement. Their job isn't done until they produce a buyer ready, willing, and able to buy. And they haven't done that until an offer has been accepted and a mortgage approval has been obtained.

WARNING 86.3:
Make sure that offers said to be cash actually are cash and aren't really mortgage preapprovals or simply negotiating ploys. If a buyer really has the cash it's worth an additional 1–2 percent reduction in your price because there's less risk— you need not worry about them getting a mortgage—and because the deal will be closed more quickly. You can separate true cash offers from phony ones by saying that you want cash payment stipulated in an otherwise unconditional contract.

TIP 86.4: If the broker comes back to you and says they simply cannot pay any more, and you're only a thousand dollars or so apart, your best response is to tell the broker that you simply cannot afford to accept the offer because you need to net a certain amount. Say you need the broker's help, and ask him or her to go back to his or her boss and ask if they can accept a lower commission. In most cases a brokerage will lower their commission to close a deal. After all, something is better than nothing. Say something along these lines: "You've done a wonderful job in negotiating this deal and I'd like to bring it to a close. But I can't without some help from your company. I need a minimum of a thousand dollars more to make this deal."

NEGOTIATE THE CONTRACT

Just because at the end of the previous stage you shook hands on a deal—a pretty good deal actually—doesn't mean the haggling is over. In fact, in many cases it has just started. Whatever deal you shook hands over now must be memorialized in a contract—a document that spells out the terms of the sale in great minutiae. This is another time when many sellers lose out due to fear. The goal of this stage is to stiffen your backbone so that, with your attorney's help, the contract for the sale of your home is a fair one.

87

Put the lawyers in touch with each other. As soon as you reach an agreement, make sure the broker passes the names, telephone numbers, and addresses of the respective attorneys to each other. Call your lawyer, tell him the agreed-upon price, and have him send the contract over to the buyer's lawyer as soon as possible, along with the request for a sit-down closing within forty-eight hours.

☐ **Done**

TIP 87.1: You're in luck if the buyers are using an attorney recommended by the broker. They will have fallen into the trap you avoided—they'll have an attorney who's more interested in closing the deal than in protecting his or her clients. For you, that's great.

WARNING 87.2: Make sure your attorney gets the proposed contract to the buyer's attorney within forty-eight hours as he or she promised. The fastest way to lose a deal is to give the buyer time to reconsider, or develop cold feet. Contracts should be hand delivered or sent via overnight mail.

88

Push for them to have an inspection done prior to the contract. It's better for both sides if the buyer has the property inspected prior to the contract. That way, any problems that need to be addressed can be handled in the contract rather than requiring separate agreements later on. This also prevents the buyer from renogiating the price after all the papers have been signed.

☐ **Done**

TIP 88.1: If the purchaser—either directly or through the broker—comes to you with any problems found in the inspection and tries to renegotiate, say something like this: "Every one of the defects in your list were considered when I finally agreed to accept your last offer." If that doesn't work, try this: "As far as I'm concerned, none of these conditions is material and they come with a house this age." If they continue to push, tell the broker to speak with your lawyer.

89

Push for a sit-down contract. A sit-down contract means that all the parties, (you, the buyer, the attorneys for both sides, and even the broker) sit down together around a table and hammer out an agreement. Lawyers hate sit-down contracts because they're put on the spot. But they're the best thing in the world for sellers.

☐ **Done**

TIP 89.1: One reason sit-down contracts are great is that they speed up the process. Once a buyer has agreed to buy a home, they begin to get scared. I call this *post purchase dissonance.* This is, after all, the single biggest purchase they'll ever make, one which they may be taking out a thirty-year loan to accomplish. The longer they have to worry, the greater the risk they'll back out.

TIP 89.2: Another reason sit-down contracts are great is that they minimize the chances of the attorneys fouling up the deal. Most deals that fall apart at this stage do so because of attorney inexperience or pomposity. One lawyer may decide to save the client from having agreed to pay too much and attempt to push through an onerous contract. Another attorney, unfamiliar with real estate transactions, may decide to apply techniques used, let's say, in criminal law to the practice of real estate law, with disastrous consequences.

90

If there's to be a mortgage contingency, make it as tight as possible. The most common condition in real estate purchase agreements is that the buyer only has to buy the property if he or she is able to obtain financing at a reasonable interest rate. If your buyer isn't paying cash you'll have to accept some form of mortgage contingency. But push for it to be as tight as possible. You want to be able to get involved in the process in case there's any problem. The buyer may object, but you're within your rights to ask for a role in the process.

☐ **Done**

WARNING 90.1: Don't go to contract unless you are reasonably sure the purchaser is financially equipped to get a mortgage. That means their income and credit are okay, and that underwriting ratios are going to be met. Have your attorney or accountant review the buyer's financial information.

CO-OP & CONDO OWNER'S TIP 90.2: Have a deadline for board approval. If the buyer will have to be accepted by a building or community board, make sure there is a tight deadline written into the contract.

91 **Be flexible with personal property.** One area which you can trade for other concessions is personal property. If you've left one or two items out of the listing—say the washer and dryer—now is the time to bring them back into play. Let's say the inspector says the oil burner is operating at only 60 percent efficiency. That may be more than sufficient, but it gives them an excuse to ask for a new one, or to ask for a price reduction. Instead, try to forestall repairs or price reductions by offering the personal property you kept out of the deal instead.

☐ **Done**

TIP 91.1: In most of these kinds of negotiations the exact financial equivalency of two items isn't as important as that both parties save face. As long as there's a mutual give-and-take the amounts don't need to be exact.

WARNING 91.2:
Some buyers and buyers' attorneys try to squeeze sellers during the contract negotiations. You have to be willing to walk right up to the edge if the buyers are being obnoxious. Realize they have just as much, if not more, to lose than you do. You will still have your house. They'll have nothing and will actually have lost their deposit.

TIP 91.3: If you find yourself reaching an impasse, ask for an adjournment and speak to the buyer directly. Suggest that the attorneys are the problem, whether or not that's the case, and that you should both speak to your respective counsels—otherwise, the deal might fall apart. This gives them a chance to save face.

92

If there are any outstanding issues, resolve them monetarily. Let's say the inspection discloses there's a cracked sidewalk. The buyer wants it repaired. Rather than agreeing to repair it, agree to a price concession, equal to the estimated cost of repairing it. Any issues left unresolved at the contract require subjective inspections prior to the closing. And if money is held aside in escrow it will be two or three times what it would actually cost to fix the problem. You want closing to be a formality, nothing more.

☐ **Done**

93

Start looking for a place to live, whether permanent or temporary. After having agreed to a price with a buyer, you can begin thinking about where you'll be moving when the deal is closed. That doesn't mean you need to go out and buy something immediately. But you do need a place to go to when you turn over the keys to this house.

☐ **Done**

94

Go through your remaining possessions. Having sold your home, you now need to realize that every object you take with you will cost you money in either storage or moving costs. Decide what you'll be taking with you and what you're willing to do without.

☐ **Done**

95

Consider holding a tag sale.
If you're parting with a considerable amount of property consider holding a tag sale. While you'll never get as much money from a tag sale as you'd wish, whatever you do make will defray the cost of moving or storing everything you are keeping.

☐ **Done**

TIP 95.1: I advise everyone who's moving to hire a professional tag sale company rather than trying to run the sale themselves. These companies are not only knowledgeable about pricing, presentation, and publicity but also have their own clientele. This is one situation where you're definitely better off leaving it to the experts.

CLOSE THE DEAL AND MOVE ON

You can breathe a sigh of relief . . . but not for too long. The rough spots are behind you. Much of what now takes place is a formality. However, that doesn't mean you have nothing to do or that there aren't potential minefields. The goal of this final stage is to make sure you're not damaged by any of those mines and that your move is a trouble-free one.

201

96

Contact moving companies.
With a date for the closing now agreed to, you can begin contacting moving companies. Call three local companies which are part of national franchises, and have them come and give you estimates.

☐ **Done**

TIP 96.1: I suggest you ask each moving company for a binding estimate. In most cases, movers will agree to provide you with a binding estimate, which they won't exceed, but which will be lowered if they've overestimated the weight of your possessions.

TIP 96.2: Speak with your insurance broker about whether or not you need extra coverage. Ask for a recommendation as to whether you should buy supplemental coverage from the mover, or on your own.

TIP 96.3: I'm in favor of having the mover do most of the packing for you. Not only are they more adept at packing than you are but also if they pack something and it breaks they're liable for the damage. If you pack it, and it breaks, they're not responsible. It's also a big time-saver. Spend your time looking for a new place and negotiating a good deal, not wrapping your collection of spoons in newspapers and searching for cardboard boxes.

97

Check on the movers' reputations. Call your local Better Business Bureau and the nearest office of the Interstate Commerce Commission to find out if there have been any complaints about the three movers you've contacted and how they have been resolved. The moving business is an easy one to enter and has more than its share of con artists.

☐ **Done**

98 Call your utility companies.

With a closing date agreed to, contact your local utility companies and ask them how service is transferred over to the new owner. In most cases they will schedule a reading for the day of the closing so you can pay the new owner for whatever energy or fuel you've used.

☐ **Done**

99

Ask your lawyer for a closing statement. Having ironed everything out at the contract meeting, your lawyer should know exactly what the two of you will need to do at the closing. Ask him or her to prepare a closing statement for you, listing exactly what you need to bring with you, including how many checks, made out to who, and in what amount. His or her fee should be included in this list.

☐ **Done**

WARNING 99.1: Make sure your attorney has resolved all title issues well in advance of the closing. He or she should also check that the purchaser is ready to accept title on time. In addition, make sure he or she has arranged for the proper documentation for paying off an existing mortgage. Generally this *payoff letter* is ordered from the mortgagee at least two weeks before the closing to insure it's ready on time.

100 Make sure the house is spotless and empty.

On the morning of the closing, the buyer will inspect the property to insure it is in the condition stipulated in the contract. Make sure it's clean and all your things are out. After the closing it's their home, not yours, and there should be no reason for you to enter it again.

☐ **Done**

101

Bring all your keys with you. Make sure you hand over all sets of keys you have to the house, garage, gates, and any outbuildings. While the buyer may end up changing all the locks, it's still important for them to feel that they, and not you, control access to the premises.

☐ **Done**

102

Resist appeals to postpone the closing Depending on how the contract is worded, you have more or less power as the seller to hold the buyer to the closing date. If the contract says the closing must be "on or about" a certain date, then it is reasonable to grant an adjournment of not more than two weeks. A contract that puts the closing on a certain date means only a small adjournment of perhaps two or three days is in order. If the contract states "time is of the essence," conditions may be attached to your accepting an adjournment. Be wary of multiple adjournments. And if you're approached about delaying closing well in advance of the date, stick to your guns and try to get the buyer to resolve his or her issues in the time frame allowed.

☐ **Done**

TIP 102.1: Be flexible about emergencies ... for a price. Of course, there can be extenuating circumstances that force a buyer to delay a closing; a medical emergency, for example. While you want to be understanding, you also want to insure it's a real emergency and not a delaying tactic. Insist that you receive additional payment equal to the interest you are losing by not having the money in your possession.

103 **Be firm if last-minute problems come up.** In some cases, buyers raise a minor issue about something they say they found during the walk-through prior to closing. Perhaps they feel that you've gotten the better of them in the negotiations and they're looking to extract some revenge. Refuse to budge. Instead, turn to the broker, who'll be sitting at the table waiting for her commission check, and tell her to handle it. Say you won't pay extortion and she has to deal with these people one way or another. The broker will either talk the buyers out of their request, or agree to pay the money out of her commission.

☐ **Done**

104

If the buyer is short of cash, turn to the broker.
Similarly, if for whatever reason the buyer ends up short of funds by some amount, turn to the broker. Say that you're willing to give the buyer time, if the broker is. If they don't get the hint, spell it out for them: It was their responsibility to provide a buyer who was ready, willing, and able to buy. Since they failed in that mission they should be willing to wait for their commission until the buyer is able to come up with the rest of the money.

☐ **Done**

TIP 104.1: If the buyer won't be there, you don't need to be there either. In some cases, buyers can't be at the closing and give their lawyer power of attorney and have him sign all the documents instead. If you learn that will be the case at your closing, you need not be there either. Give your lawyer power of attorney and let the professionals handle it on their own. You'll be paying them for the time anyway.

105

Make sure you receive a final closing statement. Within two or three weeks of the closing you should receive a final closing statement from your lawyer. It should include copies of all the documents signed at the closing and all the checks that changed hands.

☐ **Done**

106 Having sold your home, look forward, not back.

Now that the deal is done and you've handed over your keys and deposited your checks, put the house and the process behind you. Learn from your experience, but don't dwell on mistakes. You've too much to do. You've got to go out and buy another home.

☐ **Done**

TIP 106.1: For expert guidance and advice on buying your new home, pick up the companion volume to this book: *Stephen Pollan's Foolproof Guide for Buying a Home.*

GLOSSARY

adjournment: An agreement to shift a meeting or proceeding, in this case, a title closing, to a later date or time.

binding estimate: A price quote on the cost of a move in which the mover agrees that the final cost will not exceed the stated amount. While often slightly higher than other types of estimates, it insures you won't be surprised when you're handed the bill.

boilerplate: Standard legal language used in formal documents, which, while important, is rarely changed by either party since it has become the accepted form in the legal or commercial community.

buyer's booklet: A brochure, pamphlet, or handout, prepared by you for potential buyers, that contains all the information a buyer needs to make an informed decision, as well as anything that casts a good light on your home. It can be as simple as a one-page handout or as comprehensive as a ten-page bound brochure with color photographs.

closing: The meeting at which the final formalities for the sale of real estate are concluded and, after which, the buyer takes ownership and usually possession.

commission: The payment to a broker or brokerage agency for help in selling your home. The going rate is 6 percent of the selling price; however, it is entirely negotiable.

comparables or "comps": Recently sold houses or apartments, similar to yours in age, size, style, condition, and/or location, which can be used as a basis of comparison for determining price. The more recent the "comp," and the closer it resembles your home, the better its comparability.

deed: A document transferring the legal title of real estate from one person to another.

financing: The means by which a buyer will be paying the agreed price on your home if he or she doesn't have sufficient cash.

listing: The detailed physical description of your home that will be presented to potential buyers, or alternatively, the contractual relationship you have with a real estate broker for the sale of your home.

mortgage: A loan by which the borrower gives the lender a lien on real estate as security for the repayment of the loan. The borrower has use of the real estate, and the lien is removed when the loan is paid in full.

mortgage contingency: A clause in a contract for the sale of real estate that links the buyer's obligation to purchase the real estate to his or her ability to obtain a mortgage. The exact language

and restrictiveness of the clause are open
to negotiation.

mortgagor: The lender issuing a mortgage on a parcel of real estate. The borrower is called a mortgagee.

payoff letter: A document, prepared by
your mortgage holder ahead of time but
completed at the closing, which documents that you have indeed paid off your
mortgage and that the buyer or his or her
mortgage holder can now obtain title.

radon: Produced by decaying uranium,
radon is a colorless and odorless radioac-
tive gas that exists naturally in soil and
rock. It has been linked to lung cancer.
While it diffuses quickly in the open air, if
it seeps into your home it can accumulate
to potentially dangerous levels.

terms: The stipulations and details of an
agreement, including the selling price
and financing arrangements.

title: The legal right to ownership of real

estate, or alternatively, a document granting it.

title company: A company that researches and issues a report on the legal status of the title, or ownership, of your property. The report describes the property and demonstrates who owns it and whether or not there are any title defects, liens, or encumbrances that would interfere with ownership being transferred. Title companies also offer insurance protection to both owners and lenders, and in some states, may handle the entire closing.

title issues: Any matters, such as title defects, liens, or encumbrances, that could interfere with your passing title to the buyer.

underwriting ratios: The financial formula used by a lender to determine whether or not it will underwrite, or assume the risk, of making the loan. The formula may vary from lender to lender.